John Mandeville

The Voyages and Travels of Sir John Maundeville

John Mandeville

The Voyages and Travels of Sir John Maundeville

ISBN/EAN: 9783337210106

Printed in Europe, USA, Canada, Australia, Japan

Cover: Foto ©Andreas Hilbeck / pixelio.de

More available books at **www.hansebooks.com**

THE
Voyages and Travels

INTRODUCTION.

SIR JOHN MAUNDEVILLE was born at St. Albans in the beginning of the fourteenth century, and set out on his travels on Michaelmas-day, 1322. How many places he says that he visited, during an absence from home of more than thirty years, the book will tell. Rheumatic gout at last obliged him to return and rest. On his way home he showed to the Pope what he had written, in Latin, about the marvels and customs he had seen. Then, we are told, he turned his Latin book into French, and then again, in 1356, into English.

Modern criticism has made it clear that the original text was French, and only French. In the days of Maundeville Latin, French, and English were the three languages written in this country: Latin was then and long afterward the common language of the educated, and it united them into a European Republic of Letters; French was the courtly language; English was the language of the people. John Gower, the poet, Maundeville's contemporary, rested his fame upon three books, one in Latin, one in French, and one in English. The use, therefore, of French does not prove Maundeville a Frenchman. The writer says in the original French version that he *should have* written it in Latin, but had written it in French, "*jeo usse mis ceste liverette en latyn . . . mès . . jeo l'ai mys en romanz,*" which is mistranslated into the statement that he *had* written it in Latin; with the addition made by the English translator that assigns the English version to the hand of Maundeville himself. As in several places the French is mistranslated into English in a way that would have been impossible if Maundeville had been his own interpreter, and the same is true of the Latin, the most we can believe is that Maundeville wrote in French, and claimed as his own the other translations because he had caused them to be made for him. He could not have done without a Latin version if he meant to submit the book to the Pope; and he might naturally wish, when he came home, that his book should be read—as it became widely read—also in English. The oldest remaining manuscript of the book in French is dated 1371, and the oldest known MSS. of the English version can not be placed very much later. They belong, at latest, to the first quarter of the fifteenth century.

The book was planned as a guide to pilgrims to the Holy Places at Jerusalem, but, for the purpose of including as full an account of travel as could be given, roundabout ways to Jerusalem were conceived, as well as the direct way. Maundeville told facts as matter of knowledge, marvels and miracles as matter of hearsay or of faith. He said that he and his men served the Sultan of Babylon in war against the Bedouins, and had from him letters that gave admission to the least accessible of the Holy Places. He said also that for fifteen months he and his men served the great Khan in China. What he tells of Cathay and India corresponds very closely with what is to be found in the record of Friar Odoric of Pordenone, the story of whose travels in Western India and Northern China was set down in Latin just before the time of the friar's death in 1331 Maundeville's record of adventure in the Perilous Valley is, for example, borrowed from Odoric; but Maundeville's account suggests traveling companionship in that adventure with "two worthy men, friars of Lombardy." Possibly, the purpose of the book being to tell as much as possible of travel in the world as it then was, in the form of personal adventure, contributions of good matter from the books of other travelers were, for this reason, interwoven in the story of one who had traveled much himself. In whatever way he did it, Maundeville produced what became the most popular book of travel for some generations after his own time. Of no other such book, Mr. Halliwell ventured to say, "Of no book, with the exception of the Scriptures," can more MSS. be found of the end of the fourteenth and beginning of the fifteenth century. It may well be that his travelers' tales were more widely enjoyed than believed. But travelers see strange things, and have often been credited with readiness to tell more strange things than they see.

The text as here given, in modern spelling, is taken, with permission of Messrs. George Bell & Sons, from a volume of "Early Travels in Palestine," in "Bohn's Antiquarian Library." That volume includes also "Wilibald," "Sæwulf," "Benjamin of Tudela," "La Brocquiere," and "Maundrell." Here let me take occasion to say that the "Libraries," of which Henry G. Bohn began the issue forty years ago, remain a monument of well-directed zeal for cheap diffusion of true literature. The first of the volumes of "Bohn's Standard Library"—each giving about five hundred pages for three-and-sixpence, in a substantial, well-printed book—appeared on the 1st of February, 1846. Books less directly addressed to the general reader, and illustrated books, were gathered at a slightly higher price into companion "Libraries"—"Antiquarian," "Ecclesiastical," "Historical," "Classical," "Philological and Philosophical," "Scientific," "Illustrated"—and an important body of cheap literature was produced, for which every living worker in this country who draws strength from the past has reason to be grateful. In all Bohn's hundreds there is not a worthless book. We who come after him pay honor to the sturdy pioneer.

H. M.

THE PROLOGUE.

FORASMUCH as the land beyond the sea, that is to say, the Holy Land, which men call the land of promise or of behest, passing all other lands, is the most worthy land, most excellent, and lady and sovereign of all other lands, and is blessed and hallowed with the precious body and blood of our Lord Jesus Christ; in the which land it pleased him to take flesh and blood of the Virgin Mary, to environ that holy land with his blessed feet; and there he would of his blessedness shadow him in the said blessed and glorious Virgin Mary, and become man, and work many miracles, and preach and teach the faith and the law of Christian men unto his children; and there it pleased him to suffer many reprovings and scorns for us; and he that was king of heaven, of air, of earth, of sea, and of all things that are contained in them, would only be called king of that land, when he said, "*Rex sum Judeorum*," that is to say, I am king of the Jews; and that land he chose before all other lands, as the best and most worthy land, and the most virtuous land of all the world; for it is the heart and the middle of all the world; by witness of the philosopher, who saith thus, "*Virtus rerum in medio consistit;*" that is to say, "The virtue of things is in the middle;" and in that land he would lead his life, and suffer passion and death from the Jews for us, to redeem and deliver us from the pains of hell, and from death without end, which was ordained for us for the sin of our first father Adam, and for our own sins also; for, as for himself, he had deserved no evil; for he thought never evil nor did evil, and he that was king of glory and of joy might best in that place suffer death, because he chose in that land, rather than in any other, to suffer his passion and his death; for he that will publish anything to make it openly known, he will cause it to be cried and proclaimed in the middle place of a town; so that the thing that is proclaimed and pronounced may equally reach to all parts: right so, he that was creator of all the world would suffer for us at Jerusalem, that is the middle of the world, to the end and intent that his passion and his death, which was published there, might be known equally to all parts of the world.

See, now, how dearly he bought man, that he made after his own image, and how dearly he redeemed us for the great love that he had to us, and never deserved it of him. For more precious goods or greater ransom might he not put us, than his blessed body, his precious blood, and his holy life, which he inthralled for us; and he offered all for us, that never did sin. Oh! dear God! what love had he to us his subjects, when he that never trespassed would for trespassers suffer death! Right well ought we to love and worship, to dread and serve such a Lord, and to worship and praise such a holy land, that brought forth such fruit, through which every man is saved, unless it be his own fault. Well may that land be called delectable and a fruitful land, that was made moist with the precious blood of our Lord Jesus Christ; which is the same land that our Lord promised us in heritage. And in that land he would die, as seized, to leave it to us, his children.

Wherefore every good Christian man, that is of power, and hath whereof, should labor with all his strength to conquer our right heritage, and drive out all the unbelieving men. For we are called Christian men, after Christ our father. And if we be right children of Christ, we ought to claim the heritage that our father left us, and take it out of heathen men's hands. But now pride, covetousness, and envy have so inflamed the hearts of worldly lords, that they are busier to disinherit their neighbors than to claim or conquer their right heritage aforesaid. And the common people, that would put their bodies and their goods to conquer our heritage, may not do it without the lords. For an assembly of people without a chieftain, or a chief lord, is as a flock of sheep without a shepherd; the which departeth and disperseth, and know never whither to go. But would God that the temporal lords and all worldly lords were at good accord, and with the common people would take this holy voyage over the sea! Then I believe, confidently, that, within a little time, our right heritage aforesaid should be recovered, and put in the hands of the right heirs of Jesus Christ.

And forasmuch as it is long time passed that there was no general passage or voyage over the sea, and many men desiring to hear speak of the Holy Land, and have thereof great solace and comfort, I, John Maundeville, knight, albeit I be not worthy, who was born in England, in the town of Saint Albans, passed the sea in the year of our Lord Jesus Christ 1322, on the day of St. Michael; and hitherto have been a long time over the sea, and have seen and gone through many divers lands, and many provinces, and kingdoms, and isles, and have passed through Tartary, Persia, Ermony (Armenia) the Little and the Great; through Lybia, Chaldea, and a great part of Ethiopia; through Amazonia, India the Less and the Greater, a great part; and throughout many other isles that are about India; where dwell many divers folks, and of divers manners and laws, and of divers shapes of men. Of which lands and isles I shall speak more plainly hereafter. And I shall devise you some part of things that are there, when time shall be as it may best come to my mind; and especially for them that will and are in purpose to visit the holy city of Jerusalem, and the holy places that are there about. And I shall tell the way that they shall hold thither; for I have ofttimes passed and ridden the way, with good company of many lords: God be thanked!

And ye shall understand that I have put this book out of Latin into French, and translated it again out of French into English, that every man of my nation may understand it; and that lords and knights and other noble and worthy men that know Latin but little, and have been beyond the sea, may know and understand, if I err from defect of memory, and may redress it and amend it. For things passed out of long time from a man's mind or from his sight turn soon into forgetting; because a man's mind may not be comprehended or withheld, on account of the frailty of mankind.

THE VOYAGES AND TRAVELS

OF

Sir John Maundeville, Kt.

CHAPTER I.

TO TEACH YOU THE WAY OUT OF ENGLAND TO CONSTANTINOPLE.

IN the name of God, glorious and Almighty. He that will pass over the sea to go to the city of Jerusalem may go many ways, both by sea and land, according to the country that he cometh from; many ways come to one end. But you must not expect that I will tell you all the towns, and cities, and castles, that men shall go by; for then I should make too long a tale; but only some countries and the principal places that men shall go through to go the right way.

First, if a man come from the west side of the world, as England, Ireland, Wales, Scotland, or Norway, he may, if he will, go through Almaine (Germany), and through the kingdom of Hungary, which borders on the land of Polaine (Poland), and to the land of Pannonia, and so to Silesia. And the king of Hungary is a great and mighty lord, and possesses great lordships and much land. For he holds the kingdom of Hungary, Sclavonia, and a great part of Comania and Bulgaria, which men call the land of Bougres, and the realm of Russia a great part, whereof he hath made a duchy, that extendeth unto the land of Nyflan, and borders on Prussia. And we go through the land of this lord, through a city that is called Cypron, and by the castle of Neaseborough, and by the evil town, which is situated toward the end of Hungary.

And there men pass the river Danube, which is a very great river, and it goeth into Almaine, under the hills of Lombardy; and it receives forty other rivers, and runs through Hungary and through Greece, and through Thrace, and entereth into the sea, toward the east, so roughly and so sharply, that the water of the sea is fresh and keeps its sweetness twenty miles from shore.

And after, men go to Belgrave, and enter the land of Bougres; and there men pass a bridge of stone, which is upon the river Marrok And men pass through the land of Pyncemartz, and come to Greece to the city of Nye, and to the city of Fynepape, and after to the city of Adrianople, and then to Constantinople, which was formerly called Byzantium, where the Emperor of Greece usually dwells

And there is the fairest and noblest church in the world, that of St. Sophia. And before the church is the image of the Emperor Justinian, covered with gold, and he sits crowned upon a horse, and he formerly held a round apple of gold in his hand, but it is fallen down; and they say there, that it is a token that the emperor hath lost a great part of his lands and lordships For he was Emperor of Romania and of Greece, of all Asia the Less, and of the land of Syria, of the land of Judea, in which is Jerusalem, and of the land of Egypt, of Persia, and of Arabia, but he hath lost all but Greece; and men would many times restore the apple to the hand of the image, but it will not hold it. The apple betokens the lordship which he had over all the world, which is round; and the other hand he lifts up toward the east, in token to menace the misdoers. This image stands upon a pillar of marble at Constantinople.

CHAPTER II.

OF THE CROSS AND CROWN OF OUR LORD JESUS CHRIST.

At Constantinople is the Cross of our Lord Jesus Christ, and his coat without seams, and the sponge and the reed with which the Jews gave our Lord vinegar and gall on the cross; and there is one of the nails with which Christ was nailed on the cross. And some men believe that half the cross of our Lord is in Cyprus, in an abbey of monks called the Hill of the Holy Cross. But it is not so; for the cross which is in Cyprus is that on which Dismas, the good thief, was crucified.

But all men know not that, and it is an evil act; because, for profit of the offering, they say that it is the cross of our Lord Jesus Christ. And you shall understand that the cross of our Lord was made of four kinds of trees, as is contained in this verse—

"In cruce fit palma, cedrus, cypressus, oliva."

For the piece that went upright from the earth to the head was of cypress; and the piece that went across, to which his hands were nailed, was of palm; and the stock, that stood within the earth, in which was made the mortise, was of cedar; and the tablet above his head, which was a foot and a half long, on which the title was written in Hebrew, Greek, and Latin, was of olive.

And the Jews made the cross of these four kinds of trees, because they believed that our Lord Jesus Christ should have hanged on the cross as long as the cross might last; and therefore they made the foot of the cross of cedar, because cedar may not rot in earth or water; and they thought that it should have lasted long. And because they believed that the body of Christ should have stunk, therefore they made the piece that went from the earth upward of cypress, for it is well smelling, so that the smell of his body should not grieve men that passed by. And the cross-piece was of palm, because in the Old Testament it was ordained that when any one conquered he should be crowned with palm· and because they believed that they had the victory of Christ Jesus, therefore made they the cross-piece of palm. And the tablet of the title they made of olive, because olive betokens peace; and the story of Noah witnesseth that when the dove brought the branch of olive, it betokened peace made between God and man; and so the Jews expected to have peace when Christ was dead; for they said that he made discord and strife among them.

And you shall understand that our Lord was nailed on the cross in a recumbent position, and therefore he suffered the more pain. And the Christians that dwell beyond the sea, in Greece, say that the tree of the cross that we call cypress, was of that tree of which Adam eat the apple, and that they find written. And they say also, that their Scripture saith that Adam was sick, and told his son Seth to go to the angel that kept Paradise, to pray that he would send him oil of mercy to anoint his members with, that he might have health. And Seth went, but the angel would not let him come in, telling him that he might not have of the oil of mercy; but he gave him three grains of the same tree of which his father eat the apple, and bade him, as soon as his father was dead, that he should put these three grains under his tongue, and bury him so: and he did.

And of these three grains sprung a tree, as the angel said that it should, and bore a fruit, through which fruit Adam should be saved. And when Seth came again he found his father near dead. And when he was dead he did with the grains as the angel bade him; of which sprung three trees, whereof the cross was made, that bare good fruit and blessed, namely, our Lord Jesus Christ, through whom Adam, and all that come of him, should be saved and delivered from dread of death without end, unless it be by their own fault. The Jews had concealed this holy cross in the earth, under a rock of Mount Calvary; and it lay there two hundred years and more, till the time of St. Helena, the mother of Constantine, Emperor of Rome. She was the daughter of King Coel, born in Colchester, who was King of England, which was then called Britain the Greater: the Emperor Constantinus took her to wife for her beauty, and had by her Constantine, who was afterward Emperor of Rome.

And you shall understand that the cross of our Lord was eight cubits long, and the cross-piece was three cubits and a half in length. And one part of the crown of our Lord, wherewith he was crowned, and one of the nails, and the spear-head, and many other relics, are in France, in the king's chapel, the crown being placed in a vessel of crystal richly worked. For a king of France bought these relics of the Jews, to whom the emperor had given them in pledge for a great sum of silver. And if it be so, as men say, that this crown is of thorns, you shall understand that it was of rushes of the sea, which prick as sharply as thorns; for I have seen and beheld many times that of Paris and that of Constantinople; for they were both one, made of rushes of the sea. But men had divided them in two parts; of which one part is at Paris, and the other part is at Constantinople. And I have one of these precious thorns, which seems like a white thorn; and it was given to me as a great favor; for there are many of them broken and fallen into the vessel that the crown lieth in; they break for dryness, when men move it, to show it to great lords that come thither.

And you shall understand that our Lord Jesus, on the night he was taken, was led into a garden, where he was first examined very sharply; and there the Jews scorned him, and made him a crown of the branches of aubespine, or white thorn, which grew in the same garden, and set it on his head, so fast and so sore, that the blood ran down on many parts of his face, neck, and shoulders. And therefore hath white thorn many virtues; for he that beareth a branch thereof upon him, no thunder nor tempest may hurt him; and no evil spirit may enter in the house in which it is, or come to the place that it is in. And in that same garden St. Peter denied our Lord thrice.

Afterward our Lord was led forth before the bishops and the

masters of the law, into another garden belonging to Annas; and there also he was examined, reproved, and scorned, and crowned again with a white thorn, which is called barbarines, which grew in that garden, and which hath also many virtues. And afterward he was led into a garden of Caiphas, and there he was crowned with eglantine. And after he was led into the chamber of Pilate, and there he was examined and crowned. And the Jews set him in a chair, and clad him in a mantle and there they made the crown of rushes of the sea; and there they knelt to him, ard scorned him, saying, "Hail, king of the Jews!" Half of this crown is at Paris, and the other half at Constantinople. And Christ had this crown on his head when he was placed on the cross: and therefore ought men to worship it, and hold it more worthy than any of the others. And the Emperor of Almaine possess the spear-shaft, but the head of the spear is at Paris. Yet the Emperor of Constantinople saith that he hath the spear-head, and I have often seen it; but it is greater than that at Paris.

CHAPTER III.

OF THE CITY OF CONSTANTINOPLE, AND OF THE FAITH OF THE GREEKS.

At Constantinople lieth St. Anne, our Lady's mother, whom St. Helena caused to be brought from Jerusalem. And there lieth also the body of John Chrysostom, who was Archbishop of Constantinople. There lieth also St. Luke the Evangelist, whose bones were brought from Bethany, where he was buried. And many other relics are there. And there is the vessel of stone, as it were of marble, which men call Enydros, and which continually drops water, and fills itself every year, till it run over, besides what men take from within.

Constantinople is a very fair and good city, and well walled, and it is three-cornered. There is an arm of the Sea of Hellespont, which some men call the mouth of Constantinople, and some men call it the Brace (or arm) of St. George; and that arm incloses two parts of the city. And upward to the sea, upon the water, was wont to be the great city of Troy, in a very fair plain; but that city was destroyed by the people of Greece, and little thereof now appears, because it is so long since it was destroyed.

About Greece there are many isles, as Calliste, Calcas, Cetige, Tesbria, Mynea, Flaxon, Melo, Carpate, and Lemne. In this latter isle is Mount Athos, that passeth the clouds. And there are divers languages and many countries obedient to the emperor, namely Turcople, Pyneynard, Cornagne, and many others, as Thrace and Macedonia, of which Alexander was king. In this country was Aristotle born, in a city called Stagyra, a little from the city of Thrace. And at Stagyra Aristotle lieth; and there is an altar upon his tomb. And they make great feasts for him every year, as though he were a saint. And at his altar they hold their great councils and their assemblies, expecting that through inspiration of God and of him they shall have the better council.

In this country are very high hills, toward the extremity of Macedonia. And there is a great hill, called Olympus, which divides Macedonia and Thrace, so high that it passeth the clouds. And there is another hill, called Athos, so high that the shadow of it reaches to Lemne, which is an island seventy-six miles distant. At the summit of this hill the air is so clear, that no wind is found there, and therefore no animal may live there; and the air is dry.

And men say in those countries, that philosophers once went upon those hills, and held to their nose a sponge moistened with water, to have air, because the air above was so dry; and at the summit, in the dust of those hills, they wrote letters and figures with their fingers, and at the year's end they came again, and found the same letters and figures which they had written the year before, without any change. And therefore it appears evident that these hills pass the clouds and join to the pure air.

At Constantinople is the palace of the emperor, very handsome and well built; and therein is a fair place for joustings, or for other plays and sports. And it is made with stages, and hath steps about, that every man may see well, and not intercept the view of those behind. And under these stages are stables well vaulted for the emperor's horses; and all the pillars are of marble. And within the Church of St. Sophia, an emperor once would have buried the body of his father when he was dead; and, as they made the grave, they found a body in the earth, and upon the body lay a fine plate of gold, on which was written in Hebrew, Greek, and Latin, letters that said thus: " Jesus Christ shall be born of the Virgin Mary, and I believe in him." And the date when it was laid in the earth was two thousand years before our Lord was born. The plate of gold is still preserved in the treasury of the church. And they say that it was Hermogenes, the wise man.

Although the men of Greece are Christians, yet they vary from our faith; for they say that the Holy Ghost may not come of the

Son, but only of the Father. And they are not obedient to the Church of Rome, nor to the Pope; for they say that their patriarch hath as much power over the sea as the Pope hath on this side the sea. And therefore Pope John XXII. sent letters to them, how Christian faith should be all one, and that they should be obedient to the Pope, who is God's vicar on earth, to whom God gave his full power to bind and to assoil, and therefore they should be obedient to him.

But they sent back divers answers, amongst others saying thus: "We believe well that thy power is great upon thy subjects. We may not suffer thy great pride. We are not in purpose to fulfill thy great covetousness. The Lord be with thee; for our Lord is with us.—Farewell." And no other answer might he have of them. They make their sacrament of the altar of unleavened bread, because our Lord made it of such bread when he made his Maundy. And on Shere-Thursday they make their unleavened bread, in token of the Maundy, and dry it in the sun, and keep it all the year, and give it to sick men instead of God's body. And they make but one unction when they christen children. They anoint not the sick. And they say that there is no purgatory, and that the souls shall have neither joy nor pain till the day of doom.

They say, moreover, that fornication is not a deadly sin, but a thing that is according to nature; and that men and women should wed but once; and whosoever weddeth oftener than once, their children are bastards, and begotten in sin. Their priests also are wedded. They say, also, that usury is no deadly sin; and they sell benefices of holy church; and so do men in other places (God amend it when his will is!), and that is a great scandal; for now is simony king crowned in holy church; God amend it for his mercy! And they say that in Lent men shall not fast, or sing mass, except on the Saturday and on the Sunday. And they fast not on the Saturdays, except it be Christmas-eve, or Easter-eve. They suffer not the Latins to sing at their altars: and if they do by any chance, they immediately wash the altar with holy water. And they say, that there should be but one mass said at one altar upon one day. They say also that our Lord never eat, but that he made sign of eating.

They say, moreover, that we sin deadly in shaving our beards; for the beard is token of a man, and the gift of our Lord. And they say that we sin deadly in eating of animals that were forbidden in the Old Testament and by the old law, as swine, hares, and other beasts that chew not their cud And they say that we sin in eating flesh on the days before Ash-Wednesday, and in eating flesh on the

Wednesday, and eggs and cheese on the Fridays. And they curse all those who abstain from eating flesh on the Saturday. The Emperor of Constantinople appoints the patriarch, the archbishops, and the bishops, and gives the dignities and the benefices of churches, and deprives those who deserve it, when he finds any cause; and so is he lord both temporal and spiritual in his country.

And although these things touch not to our way, nevertheless they touch to that that I have promised you, to show you a part of the customs, and manners, and diversities of countries. And because this is the first country that is discordant in faith and in belief, and varies from our faith on this side the sea, therefore I have set it here, that you may know the diversity that is between our faith and theirs. For many men have great liking to hear of strange things of diverse countries.

CHAPTER IV.

ON THE WAY FROM CONSTANTINOPLE TO JERUSALEM.—OF ST. JOHN THE EVANGELIST, AND OF THE DAUGHTER OF YPOCRAS, TRANSFORMED FROM A WOMAN TO A DRAGON.

Now return I again to explain to you the way from Constantinople to Jerusalem. He that will proceed through Turkey, goes toward the city of Nice, and passes through the gate of Chienetout, and men see constantly before them the hill of Chienetout, which is very lofty; it is a mile and a half from Nice. And if you will go by water, by the Brace of St. George, and by the sea where St. Nicholas lieth, and toward many other places, first, you go to an isle that is called Sylo, in which mastic grows on small trees, out of which comes gum, as it were of plum-trees, or of cherry-trees. And after men go by the Isle of Patmos, where St. John the Evangelist wrote the Apocalypse. And you shall understand that St. John was thirty-two years of age when our Lord suffered his passion, and after his passion he lived sixty-seven years, and in the hundredth year of his age he died.

From Patmos men go to Ephésus, a fair city, and nigh to the sea. And there died St. John, and was buried in a tomb behind the high altar. And there is a fair church, for the Christians were always wont to hold that place. And in the tomb of St. John is nothing but manna, which is called angels' meat, for his body was translated into Paradise. And the Turks now hold all that place, with the city, and the church; and all Asia the Less is called Turkey. And you shall understand that St. John caused his grave to be made there in his life, and laid himself therein, all alive; and, therefore, some men say that he did not die, but that he rests there till the day of doom. And, in truth, there is a great marvel, for men may see there the earth of the tomb many times openly stir and move, as though there were living things under.

And from Ephesus we go through many islands in the sea to the city of Patera, where St. Nicholas was born, and so to Myra, where he was chosen to be bishop; and there grows very good and strong wine, which they call wine of Myra. And from thence men go to the Isle of Crete, which the emperor once gave to the Genoese.

And then we pass through the isles of Colos and of Lango, of which isles Ypocras was lord; and some men say, that in the Isle of Lango is still the daughter of Ypocras, in form and likeness of a great dragon, which is a hundred fathoms in length, as they say, for I have not seen her. And they of the isles call her lady of the land. And she lies in an old castle, in a cave, and appears twice or thrice in the year; and she doth no harm to any man unless he do her harm. She was thus changed and transformed from a fair damsel into the likeness of a dragon by a goddess named Diana; and they say that she shall remain in that form until the time that a knight come, who shall be so bold that he dare come to her and kiss her on the mouth; and then she shall turn again to her own nature, and be a woman again; but after that she shall not live long. And it is not long since a knight of Rhodes, who was bold and doughty in arms, said that he would kiss her; when he was upon his courser and went to the castle, and entered into the cave, the dragon lifted up her head toward him, and when the knight saw her in that form, so hideous and horrible, he fled away. But the dragon carried the knight upon a rock, and from thence she cast him into the sea, and so were lost both horse and man.

A young man that knew not of the dragon, went out of a ship, and proceeded through the isle until he came to the castle and entered the cave, and went so far that he found a chamber; and there he saw a damsel who was combing her head and looking in a mirror, and she had much treasure about her, and he believed she had been a woman, who dwelt there to receive men to folly; and he abode till the damsel saw the shadow of him in the mirror, and she turned her toward him and asked him, what he would? And he said, he would be her paramour. And she asked him if he were a knight? And he said, nay. And then she said that he might not be her leman; but she bade him go again unto his fellows and get him knighted, and come again upon the morrow, and she would come out of the cave before him; and then he should come and kiss her on the mouth, and have no fear, "for I shall do thee no harm, although thou see me in likeness of a dragon; for though thou see me hideous and horrible to look upon, know that it is made by enchantment. For without doubt I am no other than thou seest now, a woman, and therefore fear not; and if thou kiss me, thou shalt have all this treasure and be my lord, and lord also of all the isle."

And he departed from her and went to his fellows, in the ship, and was made a knight, and returned on the morrow to kiss the damsel. But when he saw her come out of the cave, in form of a dragon, so hideous and so horrible, he had so great fear that he fled again to the ship; and she followed him. And when she saw that he turned not again, she began to cry as a thing that had much sorrow, and then she returned to her cave; and anon the knight died. And from that time to this might no knight see her but he died anon. But when there shall come a knight who is bold enough to kiss her, he shall not die; but he shall turn the damsel into her right form and natural shape, and he shall be lord of all the countries and isles above said.

And from thence men come to the Isle of Rhodes, which isle the Hospitalers hold and govern, having on a time taken it from the emperor. It was formerly called Collos, and so the Turks call it still; and St. Paul, in his Epistles, writes to the people of this isle, *ad Colossenses*. This isle is nearly eight hundred miles from Constantinople.

From this Isle of Rhodes we go to Cyprus, where are many vines, which first produce red wine, and after one year they become white; and those wines that are most white are the clearest and best of smell. And men pass that way by a place which was a great city and a great land; and the city was called Sathalie. This city and the land were lost through the folly of a young man, who had a fair damsel whom he loved well for his paramour, and she died suddenly and was placed in a tomb of marble; and for the great love that he had to her, he went in the night to her tomb, and opened it and went in. And there came a voice to him, and said, "Go to the tomb of that woman, and open it, and if thou omittest to go thou shalt have a great harm." And he went and opened the tomb; and there came out a snake, very hideous to behold, which immediately flew about the city and the country, and soon after the city was swallowed up. And there are many perilous passages.

From Rhodes to Cyprus are five hundred miles and more; but we may go to Cyprus without touching at Rhodes. Cyprus is a very good, fair, and great island, and it hath four principal cities, with an archbishop at Nicosia, and four other bishops; and at Famagosta is one of the first harbors of the sea in the world; and there arrive Christians, Saracens, and men of all nations. In Cyprus is the hill of the Holy Cross, where there is an abbey of black monks, and there is the cross of Dismas, the good thief, as I have said before. And some men believe that there is half of the cross of our Lord; but it is not so, and they do wrong who make people believe so.

In Cyprus lies St. Zenomyne, of whom men of that country make great solemnity; and in the castle of Amours lies the body of St. Hilary, which they keep very worshipfully. Near Famagosta, St. Barnabas the apostle was born. In Cyprus they hunt with papyons, which resemble leopards, and they take wild beasts right well, and they are somewhat larger than lions, and take more sharply and more cleverly than hounds do. In Cyprus it is the custom for lords and all other men to eat on the earth; for they make trenches in the earth about in the hall, deep to the knee, and pave them; and when they will eat, they go therein and sit there. And the reason is that they may be cooler; for that land is much hotter than it is here. And at great feasts, and for strangers, they set forms and tables as men do in this country; but they themselves prefer sitting on the earth.

From Cyprus they go to the land of Jerusalem by sea, and in a day and night he that hath good wind may come to the haven of Tyre, which is now called Sur. Here was once a great and good city of the Christians; but the Saracens have destroyed it in great part; and they guard that haven carefully for fear of the Christians. Men might go more direct to that haven, without touching at Cyprus; but they go gladly to Cyprus, to rest them in the land, or to buy things that they need for their living. On the sea-side many rubies are found.

There is the well of which Holy Writ speaketh, saying, "A fountain of gardens, and a well of living waters." It was in this city of Tyre that the woman said to our Lord, "Blessed is the womb that bare Thee, and the paps which Thou hast sucked." And there our Lord forgave the woman of Canaan her sins. And before Tyre stood formerly the stone on which our Lord sat and preached, and over which was built the Church of St. Saviour.

Eight miles from Tyre, toward the east, upon the sea, is the city of Sarphen, in Sarept of the Sidonians. There dwelt Elijah the prophet, and he raised there Jonas, the widow's son, from death to life. And five miles from Sarphen is the city of Sidon, of which Dido was lady, who was wife of Eneas, after the destruction of Troy, and who founded the city of Carthage in Africa, and now it is called Didon Sayete. And in the city of Tyre reigned Agenor, the father of Dido. Sixteen miles from Sidon is Beruthe (Beirut); and from Beruthe to Sardenare is three days. And from Sardenare it is five miles to Damascus.

And those who are willing to go a long time on the sea, and come nearer to Jerusalem, may proceed from Cyprus by sea to the port of Jaffa, for that is the nearest port to Jerusalem, the distance being only one day and a half. The town is called Jaffa because one of the sons of Noah, named Japhet, founded it, and now it is called Joppa. And you shall understand that it is one of the oldest towns in the world, for it was founded before Noah's flood. And there may still be seen in the rock there the place where the iron chains were fastened, wherewith Andromeda, a great giant, was bound and put in prison, before Noah's flood; a rib of whose side, which is forty feet long, is still shown.

And those who go to the port of Tyre or Sur, before mentioned, may proceed by land, if they will, to Jerusalem. They go from Sur in a day to the city of Akoun (Acre), which was called formerly Ptolemais, and it was once a very fine city of Christians; but it is now destroyed. It stands upon the sea. From Venice to Akoun, by sea, is two thousand and eighty Lombard miles. From Calabria, or from Sicily to Akoun, by sea, is thirteen hundred Lombard miles. And the Isle of Crete is just midway. Near the city of Akoun, toward the sea, one hundred and twenty furlongs on the right, toward the south, is the hill of Carmel, where Elijah the prophet dwelt, and where the order of Friars Carmelites was first founded. This hill is not very great, nor very high.

At the foot of this hill was formerly a good city of the Christians called Caiaphas, because Caiaphas first founded it; but it is now all waste. And on the left side of the hill of Carmel is a town called Saffre, which is situated on another hill. There St. James and St. John were born, and there is a fair church in honor of them. And from Ptolemais, which is now called Akoun, it is one hundred furlongs to a great hill, called the scale (or ladder) of Tyre.

And near the city of Akoun runs a little river called Belon; and there nigh is the fosse of Memnon, which is all round; and it is one hundred cubits broad, and all full of gravel, shinging bright, of which men make fair and clear glasses. Men come from afar, by water with ships, and by land with carts, to fetch of that gravel;

and though ever so much be taken away thereof one day, on the morrow it is as full again as ever it was. And that is a great wonder. And there is always great wind in that fosse, that continually stirs the gravel and makes it troubled; and if any man put therein any kind of metal, it turns to glass, and the glass made of that gravel, if it be thrown back into the gravel, turns to gravel as it was first; and therefore some men say that it is a whirlpool of the gravelly sea.

From Akoun, above mentioned, it is four days' journey to the city of Palestine, which was of the Philistines, now called Gaza, which is a gay and rich city; and it is very fair, and full of people, and is at a little distance from the sea. From this city Samson the strong brought the gates upon a high land, when he was taken in that city; and there he slew, in a palace, the king and himself, and great numbers of the best of the Philistines, who had put out his eyes, and shaved his head, and imprisoned him by treason of Delilah, his paramour. And therefore he caused a great hall to fall upon them when they were at meat. From thence we go to the city of Cesarea, and so to the Castle of Pilgrims, and so to Ascalon, and then to Jaffa, and so to Jerusalem.

CHAPTER V.

OF MANY NAMES OF SULTANS, AND OF THE TOWER OF BABYLON.

AND he who will go by land through the land of Babylonia, where the sultan dwells commonly, he must get leave and grace of him, to go more safely through the lands and countries. And to go to the Mount of Sinai, before men go to Jerusalem, they shall go from Gaza to the castle of Daire. And after that they come out of Syria and enter a wilderness where the way is sandy; and that wilderness and desert lasts eight days. But men always find good inns and all they need of victuals. And that wilderness is called Athylec. And when a man comes out of that desert he enters into Egypt, which is called Egypt Canopac: and after other language, men call it Morsyn. And there men first find a good town, called Belethe, which is at the end of the kingdom of Aleppo; and from thence men go to Babylon and to Cairo.

At Babylon there is a fair church of our Lady, where she dwelt seven years, when she fled out of the land of Judea for dread of king Herod. And there lieth the body of St. Barbara, the virgin and martyr. And there dwelt Joseph after he was sold by his brethren.

And there Nebuchadnezzar, the king, caused the three children to be thrown into the furnace of fire because they were in the true belief; which children were called Hananiah, Azariah, Michael, as the psalm of Benedicite says. But Nebuchadnezzar called them otherwise, Shadrach, Meshach, and Abednego, that is to say, God glorious, God victorious, and God over all things and realms, on account of the miracle, that he saw God's Son go with the children through the fire, as he said. The sultan dwells in his Calahelyke (for there is commonly his residence), in a fair castle, strong and great, and well set upon a rock. In that castle dwell always, to keep it and to serve the sultan, more than 6000 persons, who receive here all necessaries from the sultan's court. I ought to know it well, for I dwelt a great while with him as soldier in his wars against the Bedouins; and he would have married me full highly to a great prince's daughter if I would have forsaken my law and my belief. But I thank God I had no will to do it for anything that he promised me.

And you shall understand that the sultan is lord of five kingdoms, that he hath conquered and taken possession of by strength; and these are their names: the kingdom of Canopac, that is Egypt; and the kingdom of Jerusalem, where David and Solomon were kings; and the kingdom of Syria, of which the city of Damascus was chief: and the kingdom of Aleppo, in the land of Mathe; and the kingdom of Arabia, that belonged to one of the three kings who made offering to our Lord when he was born. And he holds many other lands in his hand. And therewithal he holds caliphs, which is a full great thing in their language, being as much as to say, kings. And there were wont to be five sultans, but now there is no more but he of Egypt.

The first sultan was Sarocon, who was of Media (the father of Saladin), who took the caliph of Egypt and slew him, and was made sultan by strength. After him was Sultan Saladin, in whose time the King of England, Richard I., with many others, kept the passage, that Saladin might not pass. After Saladin, reigned his son Boradin; and after him his nephew. After that the Comanians, who were in slavery in Egypt, feeling themselves of great power, chose them a sultan amongst them, who took the name of Melechesalan, in whose time St. Louis, King of France, entered into the country and fought with him; and the sultan took him prisoner. This sultan was slain by his own servants. And after they chose another to be sultan, who was called Tympieman; he delivered St. Louis out of prison for a certain ransom. After him one of the

Comanians reigned, named Cachas, and slew Tympieman, in order to be sultan; he took the name of Melechemes. He was succeeded by one named Bendochdare, who slew Melechemes to be sultan, and called himself Melechdare. In his time the good King Edward of England entered into Syria, and did great harm to the Saracens. This sultan was poisoned at Damascus; and his son thought to reign after him by heritage, and took the name of Melechsache; but another, named Elphy, drove him out of the country, and made himself sultan. This man took the city of Tripoli, and destroyed many of the Christian men, in the year of Grace 1289; but he was soon after slain. Elphy's son succeeded as sultan, and took the name of Melechasseraff; he took the city of Acre, and expelled the Christians; and he also was poisoned, upon which his brother was made sultan, and called Melechnasser. And after, one who was called Guytoga took him and threw him into prison in the castle of Mount Royal, and usurped the sovereignty by force, and took the name of Melechcadelle; and he was a Tartar. But the Comanians drove him out of the country, and caused him much sorrow; and made one of themselves sultan, named Lachyn, who assumed the name of Melechmanser. One day he was playing at chess, and his sword lay beside him, and it befell that one angered him, and he was slain with his own sword. After that there was great discord before they could choose a sultan, and finally they agreed to take Melechnasser, whom Guytoga had put in prison at Mount Royal. He reigned long and governed wisely; so that his eldest son, Melechemader, was chosen after him; he was secretly put to death by his brother, who succeeded him, and was called Melechmadabron. And he was sultan when I departed from that country.

Now you must know that the sultan can lead out of Egypt more than 20,000 men of all arms; and out of Syria, and Turkey, and other countries that he holds, he may raise more than 50,000. And all these are at his wages; and they are always ready, besides the people of his country, who are without number. And each of them has six score florins by the year; but he is expected to keep three horses and a camel. And in the cities and towns are admirals, that have the government of the people. One has four to govern, another five, another more, and another a much greater number. And the admiral, himself alone, receives as much as all the other soldiers under him. And therefore, when the sultan will advance any worthy knight, he makes him an admiral. When there is dearth the knights are very poor, and then they sell both their horses and their harness.

The sultan has four wives, one Christian, and three Saracens; of whom one dwells at Jerusalem, another at Damascus, and another at Ascalon. And when they please they remove to other cities; and when the sultan will he may go and visit them. And he has as many paramours as he pleases; for he causes to be brought before him the fairest and noblest damsels of his country, who are kept and served full honorably, and he makes them all come before him, and looks at them all to see which is most to his liking, and to her anon he sends or throws a ring from his finger; and then anon she shall be bathed and richly attired, and anointed with delicate things of sweet smell, and then led to the sultan's chamber.

No stranger comes before the sultan without being clothed in cloth of gold, or of Tartary, or of Camaka, in the Saracens' guise, and according to the usage of the Saracens. And when men see the sultan for the first time, be it at the window, or in any other place, they must kneel to him and kiss the earth, for that is the manner for those who speak with the sultan to do reverence to him.

When the messengers of foreign countries come before him, the sultan's people, when the strangers speak to him, stand round the sultan with drawn swords and gysarmes and axes, their arms raised up on high with their weapons, to smite them, if they say any word that is displeasing to the sultan. Neither does any stranger come before him without receiving a promise and grant of what he asks reasonably, if it be not against his law; and so do other princes beyond. For they say that no man· should come before a prince without being the better, and departing from his presence in greater gladness than when he came before him.

You must understand that the Babylon of which I have spoken, where the sultan dwells, is not that great Babylon where the diversity of languages was first made by the miracle of God when the great tower of Babel was begun, of which the walls were sixty-four furlongs high; for that is in the great deserts of Arabia, on the way as men go toward the kingdom of Chaldea. But it is full long since any man dare approach to the tower; for it is all desert and full of dragons and great serpents, and infested by divers venomous beasts. That tower, with the city, was twenty-five miles in the circuit of the walls, as they of the country say, and as men may judge by estimation, according to what men of the country tell. And though it is called the tower of Babylon, yet there were ordained within it many mansions and great dwelling-places, in length and breadth; and it included an extensive district, for the tower alone was ten miles square.

That tower was founded by King Nimrod, who was king of that country, and he was the first king in the world. He caused an image to be made in the likeness of his father, and obliged all his subjects to worship it, in imitation of which other lords began to do the same, and this was the commencement of idols and simulacres. The town and city were situated in a fair country on a plain, which they call the country of Samar; the walls of the city were two hundred cubits in height, and fifty cubits in breadth. The River Euphrates ran through the city and about the tower; but Cyrus, King of Persia, took from them the river, and destroyed all the city and the tower also, for he divided the river into three hundred and sixty small rivers, because he had sworn that he would put the river in such point that a woman might easily pass it without taking up her clothes; because he had lost many worthy men that tried to pass the river by swimming.

And from Babylon, where the sultan dwells, to go right between the east and the north, toward the great Babylon, it is forty days across the desert. But the great Babylon is not in the land and power of the said sultan, but in the power and lordship of the King of Persia, who holds it of the Great Khan, who is the greatest emperor and the most sovereign lord of all the parts beyond; and he is lord of the isles of Cathay and of many other isles, and of a great part of India. His land borders unto Prester John's land; and he possesses so much land that he knoweth not the end of it. And he is a mightier and greater lord without comparison than the sultan. I shall speak more fully of his royal estate and of his might when I treat of India.

The city of Mechon (Mecca), where Mohammed is buried, is also in the great desert of Arabia. His body lies there very honorably in their temple, which the Saracens call mosque. It is from Babylou the Less, where the sultan dwells, to Mechon, about thirty-two days. The realm of Arabia is a very great country; but therein is overmuch desert, and no man may dwell there in that desert, for want of water, because the land is all gravelly and full of sand. And it is dry and entirely barren, because it hath no moisture, and therefore is there so much desert. And if it had rivers and wells, and the land were as in other parts, it would be as full of people and as well inhabited as in other places. For there is a great multitude of people wherever the land is inhabited.

Arabia reaches from the borders of Chaldea to the extremity of Africa, and borders on the land of Idumea, toward the end of Botron. And in Chaldea the chief city is Baldak. The chief city of Africa is Carthage, which Dido, who was Eneas's wife, founded. Mesopotamia stretches also unto the deserts of Arabia; it is an extensive country, and in it is the city of Haran, where Abraham's father dwelt, and from whence Abraham departed by command of the angel. And of that city was Ephraem, who was a celebrated scholar. Theophilus was also of that city, whom our Lady saved from the Evil One. Mesopotamia reaches from the River Euphrates to the River Tigris, lying between those two rivers; and beyond the Tigris is Chaldea, which is a very extensive kingdom.

In that realm, at Baldak abovesaid, the caliphs formerly dwelt, who were both as emperors and popes of the Arabians, lords spiritual and temporal. They were the successors of Mohammed, from whom they were descended. The city of Baldak was formerly called Sutis, and was founded by Nebuchadnezzar. There dwelt the holy prophet Daniel, and there he saw visions of heaven, and there he made the exposition of dreams. There were formerly three caliphs, and they dwelt in the city of Baldak aforesaid.

The caliph of Egypt dwelt at Cairo, beside Babylon; and at Marrok, on the west sea, dwelt the caliph of the Barbarians and Africans. But there are now none of the caliphs, nor have there been since the time of the Sultan Saladin, since which the sultan calls himself the caliph, and thus the caliphs have lost their name. You must know that Babylon the Less, where the sultan dwells, and the city of Cairo, which is near it, are great and fair cities, the one nearly adjacent to the other. Babylon is situated on the River Gyson, sometimes called the Nile, which comes out of terrestrial Paradise.

The River Nile, every year, when the sun enters the sign of Cancer, begins to increase, and continues increasing as long as the sun is in Cancer and in Leo. And it increases to such a degree that it is sometimes twenty cubits or more deep, and then it does great harm to the goods that are upon the land; for then no man can till the earth on account of its great moistness, and therefore there is dear time in that country. And also, when it increaseth little, it is dear time in that country, for want of moisture. And when the sun is in the sign of Virgo, then begins the river to wane and decrease gradually, so that when the sun is entered into the sign of Libra, then they enter between these rivers. This river comes from terrestrial Paradise, between the deserts of India; and after it descends on the earth, and runs through many extensive countries under earth; and after it comes out under a high hill, which they call Alothe, between India and Ethiopia, at a distance of five months' journey from the entrance of Ethiopia; and after it environs all Ethiopia and Mauritania, and goes all along from the land of Egypt to the city of Alexandria, to the end of Egypt, where it falls into the sea. About this river are many birds and fowls, as storks, which they call ibes.

Egypt is a long country, but it is narrow, because they may not enlarge it toward the desert for want of water. And the country is situated along the River Nile; so that that river may serve by floods or otherwise, that when it flows it may spread abroad through the country. For it raineth but little in that country, and for that cause they have no water, unless it be by the overflowing of that river. And as it does not rain the air is always pure and clear; therefore, in that country are good astronomers, for they find there no clouds to obstruct them.

The city of Cairo is very great, more extensive than that of Babylon the Less; and it is situated above toward the desert of Syria, a little above the river aforesaid. In Egypt there are two parts; Upper Egypt, which is toward Ethiopia, and Lower Egypt, which is toward Arabia. In Egypt is the land of Rameses and the land of Goshen. Egypt is a strong country, for it has many dangerous havens, because of the great rocks, that are strong and dangerous to pass by.

Toward the east of Egypt is the Red Sea, which extends to the city of Coston; and toward the west is the country of Lybia, which is a very dry land, and unfruitful, on account of the excess of heat. And that land is called Fusthe. And toward the south is Ethiopia. And toward the north is the desert, which extends to Syria. Thus the country is strong on all sides. And it is full fifteen days' journey in length, and more than twice as much of desert, and it is but two days' in breadth. Between Egypt and Nubia there is full twelve days of desert. The men of Nubia are Christians, but they are black, like the Moors, on account of the great heat of the sun.

In Egypt there are five provinces; one is called Sahythe; the other, Demeseer; another, Resithe, which is an isle in the Nile; another, Alexandria; and another, the land of Damiette. This latter city was once very strong, but it was twice taken by the Christians, and therefore the Saracens have beaten down the walls. And with the walls and the tower thereof the Saracens made another city further from the sea, and called it New Damiette, so that now the older town of Damiette is uninhabited. That city of Damiette is one of the havens of Egypt, and at Alexandria is the other. This is a very strong city; but it has no water except what is brought by conduit from the Nile, which enters into their cisterns; and if any one stopped that water from them they could not hold out a siege. In Egypt there are but few forts or castles, because the country is so strong of itself.

In Egypt is the city of Heliopolis, that is to say, the city of the Sun, in which there is a temple, made round, after the shape of the temple of Jerusalem. The priests of that temple have all their writings dated by the bird called Phenix, of which there is but one in the world. It comes to burn itself on the altar of the temple at the end of five hundred years, for so long it lives; and then the priests array their altar, and put thereon spices, and sulphur, and other things that will burn quickly, and the Phenix comes and burns itself to ashes. The next day they find in the ashes a worm; and the second day after they find a bird, alive and perfect; and the third day it flies away. This bird is often seen flying in those countries; it is somewhat larger than an eagle, and has a crest of feathers on its head greater than that of a peacock; its neck is yellow, its beak blue, and its wings of a purple color, and the tail is yellow and red. It is a very handsome bird to look at against the sun, for it shines very gloriously and nobly.

Also, in Egypt, there are gardens with trees and herbs which bear fruit seven times in the year. And in that land abundance of fair emeralds are found, which are on that account cheaper than elsewhere. When it rains, once in the summer, in the land of Egypt, the country is all full of great mires. At Cairo they sell commonly in the market, as we do beasts, both men and women of a different religion. And there is a common house in that city, which is all full of small furnaces, to which the townswomen bring their eggs of hens, geese, and ducks, to be put into the furnaces and they that keep that house cover them with horse dung, without hen, goose, or duck, or any other fowl, and at the end of three weeks or a month they come again and take their chickens and nourish them and bring them forth, so that all the country is full of them. And this they do there both winter and summer.

In that country also, and in some others, are found long apples in their season, which they call apples of Paradise; and they are very sweet and of good savor. And though you cut them in ever so many slices or parts, across or endwise, you will always find in the middle the figure of the holy cross. But they will rot within eight days, for which reason they can not be carried to far countries. They have great leaves, a foot and a half long, and proportionately broad. They find there also the apple tree of Adam, the fruit of which has a bite on one side. And there are also fig-trees which bear no leaves, but figs grow upon the small branches; and men call them figs of Pharaoh. Also near Cairo is the field where balm grows; it comes out on small trees, that are no higher than the girdle of a man's breeches, and resemble the wood of the wild vine. And in that field are seven wells, which our Lord Jesus Christ made with one of his feet, when he went to play with other children.

That field is not so well closed but men may enter at their will; but in the season when the balm is growing good guards are placed there, that no man dare enter. This balm grows in no other place but this; and though men bring of the plants to plant in other countries, they grow well and fair, but they bring forth no fruit; and the leaves of balm never fall. They cut the branches with a sharp flint stone, or with a sharp bone; for if any one cut them with iron, it would destroy their virtue and nature.

The Saracens call the wood *Enochbalse;* and the fruit, which resembles cubebs, they call *Abebissam;* and the liquor that drops from the branches they call *Guybalse.* They always cause that balm to be cultivated by Christians, or else it would not fructify, as the Saracens say themselves, for it hath been oftentimes proved. Men say also that balm grows in India the Greater, in that desert where the trees of the sun and moon spake to Alexander. But I have not seen it, for I have not been so far upward, because there are too many perilous passages. And you must know that a man ought to take great care in buying balm; for, if he does not know it well, he may very easily be deceived; for they sell a gum called turpentine instead of balm, putting thereto a little balm to give a good odor. And some put wax in oil of the wood of the fruit of balm, and say that it is balm; and some distill cloves of gilofre and spikenard of Spain, and other spices that are well smelling, and the liquor from it they call balm; and they imagine they have balm, but they are mistaken. For the Saracens counterfeit it to deceive the Christians, as I have seen many a time; and after them, the merchants and the apothecaries counterfeit it again, and then it is less worth, and a great deal worse.

But I will show how you may know and prove it, to the end that you shall not be deceived. First, you must know that the natural balm is very clear, of citron color, and strong smell; and if it be thick, or red, or black, it is counterfeit. And if you will put a little balm in the palm of your hand toward the sun, if it be fine and good you will not be able to bear your hand in the sun's heat. Also, take a little balm with the point of a knife, and touch it to the fire, and if it burn it is a good sign. Take also a drop of balm, and put it into a dish, or in a cup, with milk of a goat, and, if it be natural balm, anon it will take and curdle the milk. Or put a drop of balm in clear water, in a cup of silver or in a clean basin, and stir it well with the clear water; and if the balm be fine and genuine the water will not be troubled; but if the balm be counterfeit the water will become troubled immediately. Also, if the balm be fine, it will fall to the bottom of the vessel, as though it were quicksilver; for the fine balm is twice as heavy as the balm that is counterfeited.

Now I will speak of another thing that is beyond Babylon, above the Nile, toward the desert, between Africa and Egypt; that is, of the granaries of Joseph, that he caused to be made, to keep the grains against the dear years. They are made of stone, well made by masons' craft; two of them are marvelously great and high, the others are not so great. And each granary has a gate to enter within, a little above the earth; for the land is wasted and fallen since the granaries were made. Within they are all full of serpents; and above the granaries without are many writings in divers languages. And some men say that they are sepulchers of great lords that were formerly; but that is not true, for all the common rumor and speech of the people there, both far and near, is that they are the granaries of Joseph; and so find they in their writings and chronicles. On the other side, if they were sepulchers, they would not be empty within; for you may well know, that tombs and sepulchers are not made of such magnitude or elevation; wherefore it is not credible that they are tombs or sepulchers.

Now I will proceed to tell you the other ways that draw toward Babylon, where the sultan dwells, which is at the entry of Egypt; because many people go thither first, and after that to Mount Sinai, and then return to Jerusalem, as I have told you before. For they perform first the longer pilgrimage, and return by the nearest ways; because the nearer way is the more worthy, and that is Jerusalem; for no other pilgrimage is to be compared to it. But to accomplish their pilgrimages more easily and safely, men go first the longer way. But whoever will go to Babylon by another way, and shorter from the countries of the west, he may go by France, Burgundy, and Lombardy. It is not necessary to tell you the names of the cities and towns in that way, for the way is common, and known to everybody.

There are many ports where men take the sea; some embark at Genoa; some at Venice, and pass by the Adriatic Sea, which is called the Gulf of Venice, and divides Italy and Greece on that side;

and some go to Naples; some to Rome, and from Rome to Brindes, and embark there, and in many other places. Some go by Tuscia, Campania, Calabria, by Apulia, and by the mountains of Italy Chorisque, by Sardinia, and by Sicily, which is a great and good isle. In that isle of Sicily is a kind of garden, in which are many different fruits; and the garden is green and flourishing at all seasons of the year, as well in winter as in summer. The isle contains in compass about three hundred and fifty French miles. Between Sicily and Italy there is but a little arm of the sea, which men call the Faro of Messina; and Sicily is between the Adriatic Sea and the Sea of Lombardy. From Sicily to Calabria is but eight Lombard miles.

In Sicily there is a kind of serpent by which men assay and prove if their children be bastards or not; for if they are born in lawful marriage, the serpents go about them, and do them no harm; but if they are illegitimate, the serpents bite them and kill them with their venom; and thus many wedded men ascertain if the children be their own. Also in that isle is Mount Etna, which men call Mount Gybell, and volcanoes, that are ever burning. And there are seven places which burn and cast out flames of divers colors; and by the changing of those flames, men of that country know when it will be dearth or good time, or cold or hot, or moist or dry, or in all other manners how the time will vary. From Italy to the volcanoes is but twenty-five miles; and they say that the volcanoes are ways to hell.

Also, for those who go by Pisa, there is an arm of the sea, where men go to other havens in those parts, and then they pass by the isle of Greaf, that is at Genoa; and so they arrive in Greece at the port of the city of Myrok, or at the port of Valone, or at the city of Duras (where there is a duke), or at other ports in those parts; and so men go to Constantinople. And afterward they go by water to the Isle of Crete, and to the Isle of Rhodes, and so to Cyprus, and so to Athens, and from thence to Constantinople.

To hold the more direct way by sea, it is full one thousand eight hundred and eighty Lombard miles. And after, from Cyprus they go by sea, and leave Jerusalem and that country on the left, and proceed to Egypt, and arrive at the city of Damiette, at the entrance of Egypt, whence they go to Alexandria, which is also upon the sea. In that city was St. Catharine beheaded; and there St. Mark the Evangelist was martyred and buried; but the Emperor Leo caused his bones to be carried to Venice.

There is still at Alexandria a fair church, all white, without pictures; and so are all the other churches which belonged to the Christians all white within, for the Pagans and the Saracens whitewashed them, to destroy the images of saints that were painted on the walls. The city of Alexandria is fully thirty furlongs in length, but it is but ten broad; and it is a noble and fair city. Here the river Nile enters the sea; in which river are found many precious stones, and much also of lignum aloes, a kind of wood that comes out of terrestrial Paradise, and is good for many different medicines; and it is very precious. From Alexandria we go to Babylon, where the sultan dwells, which is situated also on the river Nile; and this is the shortest way to go direct to Babylon.

From Babylon to Mount Sinai, where St. Catherine lieth, you must pass by the desert of Arabia, by which Moses led the people of Israel; and then you pass the well which Moses made with his hand in the desert, when the people murmured because they found nothing to drink. And then you pass the well of Marah, of which the water was first bitter, but the children of Israel put therein a tree, and anon the water was sweet and good to drink. And then you go by the desert to the Vale of Elim, in which vale are twelve wells; and there are seventy-two palm-trees that bear the dates which Moses found with the children of Israel. And from that valley is but a good day's journey to Mount Sinai.

And those who will go by another way from Babylon go by the Red Sea, which is an arm of the ocean. There Moses passed with the children of Israel across the sea all dry, when Pharaoh, King of Egypt, pursued him. That sea is about six miles broad. That sea is not redder than other seas; but in some places the gravel is red, and therefore they call it the Red Sea. That sea runs to the borders of Arabia and Palestine, its extent being more than four days. Then we go by desert to the Vale of Elim, and thence to Mount Sinai. And you must know that by this desert no man may go on horseback, because there is neither meat for horses nor water to drink; wherefore they pass that desert with camels. For the camel finds always food in trees and on bushes, and he can abstain from drink two or three days, which no horse can do.

From Babylon to Mount Sinai is twelve good days' journey, and some make it more; and some haste them, and thus make it less. And men always find interpreters to go with them in the countries, and further beyond, until they know the language. Travelers must carry with them victuals and other necessaries sufficient to last through those deserts.

Mount Sinai is called the Desert of Sin, that is to say, the burn ing bush; because there Moses saw our Lord God many times in form of fire burning upon that hill, and also in a burning bush, and spake to him. And that was at the foot of the hill. There is an abbey of monks, well built and well closed with gates of iron for fear of wild beasts. The monks are Arabians or Greeks; and there is a great convent, and they are all as hermits, and drink no wine except on principal feasts; they are very devout men, and live in poverty and simplicity on gourds and dates, and perform great abstinence and penance.

Here is the Church of St. Catharine, in which are many lamps burning, for they have enough oil of olives both to burn in their lamps, and to eat also, which plenty they have by God's miracle; for the ravens, crows, and choughs, and other fowls of that country, assemble there once every year, and fly thither as in pilgrimage; and each brings a branch of bays or olive in its beak, instead of offering, and leaves it there; of which the monks make great plenty of oil; and this is a great marvel. And since fowls that have no natural knowledge or reason go thither to seek that glorious Virgin, well more ought men to seek her and worship her. Behind the altar of that church is the place where Moses saw our Lord God in a burning bush. When the monks enter that place they always put off both hose and shoes or boots, because our Lord said to Moses, "Put off thy shoes from off thy feet, for the place whereon thou standest is holy ground." And the monks call that place Bezeleel, that is, the shadow of God.

Beside the high altar, raised on three steps, is the chest of alabaster containing the bones of St. Catharine, and the prelate of the monks shows the relics to the pilgrims, and rubs the bones with an instrument of silver, whereupon there issues a little oil, as though it were a kind of sweating, which is neither like oil nor balm, but is very sweet of smell; and of that they give a little to the pilgrims, for there issues but a small quantity of the liquor. They next show the head of St. Catharine, and the cloth that she was wrapped in, which is still all bloody. And in that same cloth, so wrapped, the angels bore her body to Mount Sinai, and there buried her with it. They also show the bush which burned and was not consumed, in which our Lord spake to Moses; and they have many other relics.

When the prelate of the abbey is dead, I have been informed that his lamp becomes extinguished. And when they choose another prelate, if he be a good man and worthy to be prelate, his lamp will light by the grace of God, without being touched by any man. For every one of them has a lamp for himself, and by their lamps they know well when any of them shall die, for then the light begins to change and wax dim. And if he be chosen to be prelate, and it is not worthy, his lamp immediately goes out. Other men have told me that he that sings the mass for the prelate that is dead finds written upon the altar the name of him that shall be chosen prelate. One day I asked several of the monks how this befell. But they would not tell me, until I said that they ought not to hide the grace that God did them, but that they should publish it, to make the people have the more devotion, and that they sinned in hiding God's miracle, as appeared to me. And then they told me that it so happened often; but more I might not have of them.

In that abbey no flies, toads, or lizards, or such foul venomous beasts, nor lice, nor fleas, ever enter, by the miracle of God and of our Lady; for there were wont to be so many such kind of pests, that the monks were resolved to leave the place, and were gone thence to the mountain above, to eschew that place. But our Lady came to them and bade them return; and since that time such vermin have never entered in any place amongst them, nor never shall enter hereafter. Before the gate is the well where Moses smote the stone from which the water came out abundantly.

From that abbey you go up the mountain of Moses by many steps; and there is, first, a church of our Lady where she met the monks when they fled away from the vermin just mentioned; and higher up the mountain is the chapel of Elijah the prophet, which place they call Horeb, whereof Holy Writ speaks, "And he went in the strength of that meat forty days and forty nights, unto Horeb the mount of God." And close by is the vine that St. John the Evangelist planted; and a little above is the chapel of Moses, and the rock where Moses fled for dread when he saw our Lord face to face. And in that rock is imprinted the form of his body; for he threw himself so strongly and so hard on that rock that all his body was buried into it, through the miracle of God And near it is the place where our Lord gave to Moses the ten commandments of the law. And under the rock is the cave where Moses dwelt when he fasted forty days and forty nights.

And from that mountain you pass a great valley, to go to another mountain, where St. Catharine was buried by the angels of our Lord; in which valley is a church of forty martyrs, where the monks of the abbey often sing. That valley is very cold. Next you go up the mountain of St. Catharine, which is higher than the mount of Moses; and there, where St. Catharine was buried, is neither church nor chapel, nor other dwelling-place; but there is a heap of stones about the place where her body was placed by the angels. There was formerly a chapel there, but it was cast down, and the stones lie still scattered about. And although the Collect of St. Catharine says that it is the place where our Lord gave the ten commandments to Moses, and where the blessed virgin St. Catharine was buried, we are to understand this as meaning that it is the same country, or in a place bearing the same name; for both hills are called the Mount of Sinai; but it is a great way from one to the other, and a great deep valley lies between them.

CHAPTER VI.

OF THE DESERT BETWEEN THE CHURCH OF ST. CATHARINE AND JERUSALEM.—OF THE DRY TREE; AND HOW ROSES FIRST CAME INTO THE WORLD.

AFTER people have visited these holy places, they proceed toward Jerusalem, having taken leave of the monks and recommended themselves to their prayers. And then the monks give the pilgrims victuals to pass the desert toward Syria, which desert extends full thirteen days' journey. In that desert dwell many of the Arabians, who are called Bedouins and Ascopardes, who are people full of all evil conditions, having no houses, but tents, which they make of the skins of camels and other beasts that they eat; and under these they sleep and dwell, in places where they can find water, as on the Red Sea or elsewhere; for in that desert there is great want of water, and it often happens that where men find water at one time in a place, there is none at another time; and for that reason they make no habitations there.

These people do not till the ground nor labor; for they eat no bread, except it be those who dwell near a good town, who go thither and eat bread sometimes. They roast their flesh and fish on the hot stones in the sun; and they are strong and warlike men, and there is so great a multitude of them that they are without number. Their only occupation is to hunt animals for their food. They care not for their lives, and therefore they fear not the sultan nor any other prince; but dare to war with all princes who do the many grievance; and they are often at war with the sultan, as they were at the time I was with him. They carry but one shield and one spear, without other arms; they wrap their heads and necks with a great quantity of white linen cloth, and they are right felonious and foul, and of a cursed nature.

When you pass this desert, on the way to Jerusalem, you come to Beersheba, which was formerly a very fair and pleasant town of the Christians, some of whose churches still remain. In that town Abraham the Patriarch dwelt a long time. It was founded by Beersheba (Bathsheba), the wife of Sir Uriah, the knight, on whom King David begat Solomon the Wise, who was king, after David, over the twelve tribes of Jerusalem, and reigned forty years. From thence we go to the city of Hebron, a distance of two good miles; it was formerly called the Vale of Mamre, and sometimes the Vale of Tears, because Adam wept there a hundred years for the death of Abel, his son, whom Cain slew.

Hebron was the principal city of the Philistines, and was inhabited some time by giants. And it was a sacerdotal city, that is, a sanctuary, of the tribe of Judah; and was so free, that all manner of fugitives from other places for their evil deeds, were received there. In Hebron Joshua, Calephe, and their company, came first to espy how they might win the land of promise. Here King David first reigned, seven years and a half; and in Jerusalem he reigned thirty-three years and a half. In Hebron are all the sepulchers of the patriarchs, Adam, Abraham, Isaac, and Jacob; and their wives Eve, Sarah, Rebecca, and Leah; which sepulchers the Saracens keep very carefully, for they hold the place in great reverence, on account of the holy fathers, the patriarchs, that lie there. And they suffer no Christian to enter that place, except by special grace of the sultan; for they hold Christians and Jews as dogs, and say that they should not enter into so holy a place. And they call that place where they lie Double Spelunk, or Double Cave, or Double Ditch, because the one lies above the other And the Saracens call the place in their language Karicarba, that is, the Place of Patriarchs. The Jews call it Arbothe.

And in that same place was Abraham's house, and there he sat and saw three persons, and worshiped but one: as Holy Writ saith, *He saw three and worshiped one;* and at the same place Abraham received the angels into his house. Close by that place is a cave in the rock, where Adam and Eve dwelt when they were put out of Paradise, and there they begat their children. And in that same place was Adam formed and made, as some men say; for they used to call that place the Field of Damascus, because it was in the lordship of Damascus. And from thence he was translated into Paradise, as they say; and after he was driven out of Paradise he was left there.

Here begins the Vale of Hebron, which extends nearly to Jerusalem. There the angel commanded Adam that he should dwell with his wife Eve, on whom he begat Seth, of which tribe Jesus Christ was born. In that valley is a field where men draw out of the earth a thing they call cambylle, which they eat instead of spice, and they carry it to sell. And men may not make the hole where it is taken out of the earth so deep or wide, but at the year's end it is full again up to the sides, through the grace of God.

Two miles from Hebron is the grave of Lot, Abraham's brother. And a little from Hebron is the mount of Mamre, from which the valley takes its name. And there is an oak-tree which the Saracens call dirpe, which is of Abraham s time; and people call it the dry tree. They say that it has been there since the beginning of the world, and that it was once green and bore leaves, till the time that our Lord died on the cross, and then it dried; and so did all the trees that were then in the world. And there is a prophecy, that a lord, a prince of the west side of the world, shall win the Land of Promise, that is, the Holy Land, with the help of the Christians; and he shall cause Mass to be performed under that dry tree, and then the tree shall become green and bear both fruit and leaves. And through that miracle many Saracens and Jews shall be converted to the Christian faith. And, therefore, they do great worship thereto, and guard it very sedulously. And although it be dry, still it has great virtue; for, certainly, he that hath a little thereof upon him, it heals him of the falling evil, and his horse shall not be afoundered; and many other virtues it hath, on account of which it is highly esteemed.

From Hebron we proceed to Bethlehem, in half a day, for it is but five miles; and it is a very fair way, by pleasant plains and woods. Bethlehem is a little city, long and narrow, and well walled, and on each side inclosed with good ditches. It was formerly called Ephrata, as Holy Writ says, "Lo, we heard it at Ephrata." And toward the east end of the city is a very fair and handsome church, with many towers, pinnacles, and corners strongly and curiously made; and within are forty-four great and fair pillars of marble. And between the city and the church is the Field *Floridus*, that is to say, the field flourished; for a fair maiden was blamed with wrong, and slandered, that she had committed fornication, for which cause she was condemned to be burned in that place; and as the fire began to burn about her, she made her prayers to our Lord, that as truly as she was not guilty, He would by His merciful grace help her, and make it known to all men. And when she had thus said, she entered into the fire, and immediately the fire was extinguished, and the faggots that were burning became red rosebushes, and those that were not kindled became white rosebushes, full of roses. And these were the first rose-trees and roses, both white and red, that ever any man saw. And thus was this maiden saved by the grace of God. And therefore is that field called the field that God flourished, for it was full of roses.

Also near the choir of the church, at the right side, as men go down sixteen steps, is the place where our Lord was born; which is full well made of marble, and full richly painted with gold, silver, azure, and other colors. And three paces from it is the crib of the ox and the ass. And beside that is the place where the star fell, which led the three kings, Jaspar, Melchior, and Balthazar; but the Greeks call them Galgalathe, Malgalathe, and Saraphie; and the Jews call them in Hebrew Appelius, Amerrius, and Damasus. These three kings offered to our Lord gold, incense, and myrrh; and they met together by a miracle of God, for they met together in a city in India called Cassak, which is fifty-three days' from Bethlehem, and yet they arrived at Bethlehem on the thirteenth day, which was the fourth day after they had seen the star, when they met in that city; and thus they were nine days from that city to Bethlehem; and that was a great miracle.

Also, under the cloister of the church, by eighteen steps at the right side, is the charnel-house of the Innocents, where their bones lie. And before the place where our Lord was born is the tomb of St. Jerome, who was a priest and cardinal, and translated the Bible and Psalter from Hebrew into Latin; and without the church is the chair that he sat in when he translated it. And close by that church, at a distance of sixty fathoms, is a church of St. Nicholas, where our Lady rested after she was delivered of our Lord. And forasmuch as she had too much milk in her breasts, which grieved her, she milked them on the red stones of marble; so that the traces may yet be seen all white in the stones.

And you must understand that all who dwell in Bethlehem are Christians. And there are fair vineyards about the city, and great plenty of wine, which the Christians make.

But the Saracens neither cultivate vines nor drink wine; for their books of their law, that Mohammed gave them, which they call their Alkoran, (and some call it Mesaphe, and in another language it is called Harme), forbids them to drink wine. For in that book Mohammed cursed all who drink wine, and all who sell it. For some men say that he slew once a hermit, whom he loved much, in his drunkenness; and therefore he cursed wine and them that drink it. And also, the Saracens breed no pigs and they eat no swine's flesh, for they say it is brother to man, and it was forbidden by the old law; and they hold all accursed who eat thereof. Also in the land of Palestine and in the land of Egypt, they eat but little or no veal or beef, except when the animal is old, that he may work no more; for it is forbidden, because they have but few of them, and they keep them to plow their lands. In this city of Bethlehem was David the king born, and he had sixty wives; and the first wife was called Michal; and also he had three hundred concubines.

From Bethlehem to Jerusalem it is but two miles. And in the way to Jerusalem, half a mile from Bethlethem, is a church, where the angels announced to the shepherds the birth of Christ. And in that way is the tomb of Rachel, the mother of Joseph the patriarch, who died immediately after she was delivered of her son Benjamin; and there she was buried by Jacob, her husband, and he caused twelve great stones to be placed over her, in token that she had borne twelve children. In the same way, half a mile from Jerusalem, the star appeared to the three kings. In that way also are many churches of Christians, by which men go towards the city of Jerusalem.

CHAPTER VII.

OF THE PILGRIMAGES IN JERUSALEM, AND OF THE HOLY PLACES THEREABOUT.

JERUSALEM, the holy city, stands full fair between hills; and there are no rivers or wells, but water comes by conduit from Heron. And you must know that Jerusalem of old, until the time of Melchisedek, was called Jebus; and afterward it was called Salem, until the time of King David, who put these two names together, and called it Jebusalem; and after that King Solomon called it Jerosoluma; and after that it was called Jerusalem, and so it is called still. Around Jerusalem is the kingdom of Syria; and there beside is the land of Palestine; and beside it is Ascalon; and beside that is the land of Maritaine.

But Jerusalem is in the land of Judea; and it is called Judea, because Judas Maccabeus was king of that country. And it borders eastward on the kingdom of Arabia; to the south, on the land of Egypt; to the west, on the great sea; and to the north, toward Syria, on the sea of Cyprus. In Jerusalem was formerly a patriarch, with archbishops and bishops about in the country. Around Jerusalem are these cities: Hebron, seven miles; Jericho, six miles; Beersheba, eight miles; Ascalon, seventeen miles; Jaffa, sixteen miles; Ramatha, three miles; and Bethlehem, two miles. And two miles from Bethlehem, toward the south, is the church of St. Karitot, who was abbot there; for whom they made great lamentation among the monks when he died; and they continue still in mourning in the manner that they made their lamentation for him the first time; and it is very sad to behold.

This country and land of Jerusalem hath been in the hands of many different nations, and often therefore hath the country suffered much tribulation for the sin of the people that dwell there. For that country hath been in the hands of all nations; that is to say, of Jews, Canaanites, Assyrians, Persians, Medes, Macedonians, Greeks, Romans, Christians, Saracens, Barbarians, Turks, Tartars, and of many other different nations; for God will not let it remain long in the hands of traitors or of sinners, be they Christians or others. And now the heathens have held that land in their hands forty years and more; but they shall not hold it long, if God will.

When men come to Jerusalem, their first pilgrimage is to the Church of the Holy Sepulcher, where our Lord was buried, which is without the city on the north side; but it is now inclosed by the town wall. And there is a very fair church, round, and open above, and covered in its circuit with lead; and on the west side is a fair and high tower for bells, strongly made; and in the middle of the church is a tabernacle, as it were a little house, made with a little low door; and that tabernacle is made in manner of half a compass, right curiously and richly made of gold and azure and other rich colors.

And in the right side of that tabernacle is the sepulcher of our Lord; and the tabernacle is eight feet long, and five wide, and eleven in height; and it is not long since the sepulcher was all open, that men might kiss it and touch it. But because pilgrims that came thither labored to break the stone in pieces or in powder, therefore the sultan has caused a wall to be made round the sepulcher, that no man may touch it.

In the left side of the wall of the tabernacle, about the height of a man, is a great stone, the magnitude of a man's head, that was of the holy sepulcher; and that stone the pilgrims come thither kiss. In that tabernacle are no windows; but it is all made light with lamps which hang before the sepulcher. And there is one lamp which hangs before the sepulcher which burns bright; and on Good Friday it goes out of itself, and lights again by itself at the hour that our Lord rose from the dead. Also, within the church, at the right side, near the choir of the church, is Mount Calvary, where our Lord was placed on the cross. It is a rock of a white color, a little mixed with red; and the cross was set in a mortise in the same rock; and on that rock dropped the blood from the wounds of our Lord when he was punished on the cross; and that is called Golgotha. And they go up to that Golgotha by steps; and in the place of that mortise Adam's head was found, after Noah's flood, in token that the sins of Adam should be redeemed in that same place. And upon that rock Abraham made sacrifice to our Lord.

And there is an altar, before which lie Godfrey de Boulogne and Baldwin, and other Christian kings of Jerusalem; and near where our Lord was crucified is this written in Greek: "'Ο Θεὸς Βασιλεὺς ἡμῶν πρὸ αἰώνων εἰργάσατο σωτηρίαν ἐν μέσῳ τῆς γῆς·"—that is to say, in Latin, "*Deus rex noster ante secula operatus est salutem in medio terræ;*" in English, "God our king, before the worlds, hath wrought salvation in the midst of the earth." And also on the rock where the cross was set are written, within the rock, these words: "Ὁ εἶδεις, ἐστὶ βάσις τῆς πίστεως ὅλης τοῦ κόσμου τούτου·"—that is to say, in Latin, "*Quod vides, est fundamentum totius fidei hujus mundi;*" in English, "What thou seest is the ground of all the faith of this world." And you shall understand that when our Lord was placed on the cross he was thirty-three years and three months old.

Also, within Mount Calvary, on the right side, is an altar, where the pillar lieth to which our Lord Jesus was bound when he was scourged; and there, besides, are four pillars of stone that always drop water; and some men say that they weep for our Lord's death. Near that altar is a place under earth, forty-two steps in depth, where the holy cross was found by the wisdom of St. Helena, under a rock where the Jews had Lid it. And thus was the true cross assayed; for they found three crosses, one of our Lord, and two of the two thieves; and St. Helena placed a dead body on them, which arose from death to life when it was laid on that on which our Lord died. And thereby, in the wall, is the place where the four nails of our Lord were hid; for he had two in his hands and two in his feet; and of one of these the Emperor of Constantinople made a bridle to his horse to carry him in battle; and through virtue thereof he overcame his enemies, and won all the land of Lesser Asia, that is to say, Turkey, Armenia the Less and the Greater, and from Syria to Jerusalem, from Arabia to Persia, from Mesopotamia to the kingdom of Aleppo, from Upper and Lower Egypt, and all the other kingdoms, unto the extremity of Ethiopia, and into India the Less, that was then Christian.

And there were, in that time, many good holy men, and holy hermits, of whom the Book of Lives of Fathers speaks; but they are now in the hands of Pagans and Saracens. But when God Almighty will, as the lands were lost through sin of the Christians, so shall they be won again by Christians through help of God. And in the midst of that church is a compass, in which Joseph of Arimathea laid the body of our Lord when he had taken Him down from the cross; and there he washed the wounds of our Lord. And that compass, men say, is the middle of the world.

And in the Church of the Sepulcher, on the north side, is the place where our Lord was put in prison (for He was in prison in many places); and there is a part of the chain with which He was bound; and there He appeared first to Mary Magdalene when He was risen, and she thought that He had been a gardener. In the Church of St. Sepulcher there were formerly canons of the order of St. Augustin, who had a prior, but the patriarch was their head. And outside the doors of the church, on the right side, as men go upward eighteen steps, is the spot where our Lord said to His mother, "Woman, behold thy son!" And after that He said to John, His disciple, "Behold thy mother!" And these words he said on the cross.

And on these steps went our Lord when He bare the cross on his shoulder. And under these steps is a chapel; and in that chapel sing priests of India, not after our law, but after theirs; and they always make their sacrament of the altar, saying *Pater noster*, and other prayers therewith, with which prayers, they say the words that the sacrament is made of; for they know not the additions that many popes have made; but they sing with good devotion. And near there is the place where our Lord rested Him when He was weary for bearing of the cross. Before the Church of the Sepulcher the city is weaker than in any other part, for the great plain that is between the church and the city.

And toward the east side, without the walls of the city, is the vale of Jehoshaphat, which adjoins to the walls as though it were a large ditch. And over against that vale of Jehoshaphat, out of the city, is the Church of St. Stephen, where he was stoned to death. And there beside is the golden gate, which may not be opened, by which gate our Lord entered on Palm-Sunday, upon an ass; and the gate opened to Him, when He would go unto the temple· and the marks of the ass's feet are still seen in three places on the steps, which are of very hard stone. Before the Church of St. Sepulcher, two hundred paces to the south, is the great hospital of St. John, of which the Hospitalers had their foundation. And within the palace of the sick men of that hospital are one hundred and twenty-four pillars of stone; and in the walls of the house, besides the number aforesaid, there are fifty-four pillars that support the house. From that hospital, going toward the east, is a very fair church, which is called Our Lady the Great; and after it there is another church, very near, called our Lady the Latin; and there stood Mary Cleophas and Mary Magdalene, and tore their hair, when our Lord was executed on the cross.

CHAPTER VIII.

OF THE TEMPLE OF OUR LORD; THE CRUELTY OF KING HEROD; MOUNT SION; OF PROBATICA PISCINA, AND NATATORIUM SILOÆ.

ONE hundred and sixty paces from the Church of the Sepulcher, toward the east, is the temple of our Lord. It is a very fair house, circular and lofty, and covered with lead, and well paved with white marble, but the Saracens will not suffer any Christians or Jews to come therein, for they say that no such foul sinful men should come into so holy a place; but I went in there, and in other places where I would, because I had letters of the sultan, with his great seal, and other men have commonly but his signet.

In these letters he commanded, of his special grace, to all his subjects, to let me see all the places, and to inform me fully of all the mysteries of every place, and to conduct me from city to city if necessary, and to receive me and my company courteously, and obey all my reasonable requests if they were not contrary to the royal power and dignity of the sultan or of his law. And to others, who have served him and ask him grace, he gives only his signet, which they cause to be borne before them, hanging on a spear, and the people of the country do great worship and reverence to his signet or his seal, and kneel thereto as lowly as we do to the procession of the Host. But they show much greater reverence to his letters, for the admiral, and all other lords to whom they are shown, kneel down before they receive them, and then they take them and put them on their heads, and after they kiss them, and then they read them, kneeling with great reverence; and then they offer themselves to do all the bearer asks. And in this temple of our

Lord were formerly canons regular, who had an abbot to whom they were obedient.

You must know that this is not the temple that Solomon made, which lasted only one thousand one hundred and two years. For Titus, the son of Vespasian, Emperor of Rome, had laid siege about Jerusalem to overcome the Jews, because they put our Lord to death without the emperor's leave. And when he had won the city he burned the temple and beat it down and all the city, and took the Jews, and put to death one million one hundred thousand of them; and the others he put in prison, and sold them to slavery, thirty for a penny, because they said they bought Jesus for thirty pennies; and he sold them cheaper, giving thirty for one penny.

After that Julian the Apostate, when emperor, gave the Jews permission to make the temple of Jerusalem, for he hated the Christians, although he had been christened; but he forsook his law, and became a renegade. And when the Jews had made the temple an earthquake came and cast it down (as God would), and destroyed all that they had made. And after that, Hadrian, who was Emperor of Rome, and of the lineage of Troy, rebuilt Jerusalem and the temple, in the same manner as Solomon made it. And he would not suffer Jews to dwell there, but only Christians. For although he was not christened, yet he loved Christians more than any other nation, except his own. This emperor caused the Church of St. Sepulcher to be inclosed within the city walls; before, it was without the city. And he would have changed the name of Jerusalem, and called it Ælia, but that name lasted not long.

The Saracens continue to show much reverence to that temple, and say that the place is very holy. And when they go in they go barefooted, and kneel many times. And when my fellows and I saw that, when we came in we took off our shoes, and entered barefooted, and thought we would do as much worship and reverence there as any of the misbelieving men, with as great compunction of heart. This temple is sixty-four cubits wide, and as many in length, and a hundred and twenty cubits high; and within it has pillars of marble all round; and in the middle of the temple are many high stages, fourteen steps high, with good pillars all about, and this place the Jews call the Holy of holies. No man, except the Prelate of the Saracens, who makes their sacrifice, is allowed to come in there. And the people stand all about, in divers stages, according to their dignity, or rank, so that they may all see the sacrifice.

And in that temple are four entrances, with gates of cypress, well made and curiously wrought. Within the east gate is the place where our Lord said, " Here is Jerusalem." And on the north side of the temple, within the gate, there is a well, but it does not run; of this Holy Writ speaks, and says, " I saw water come out of the temple." And on the other side of the temple there is a rock which men call Moria, but after it was called Bethel, where the ark of God, with relics of Jews, was wont to be put.

That ark or hutch, with the relics, Titus carried with him to Rome, when he had overthrown the Jews; it contained the ten commandments, Aaron's rod, and that of Moses, with which he made the Red Sea divide as it had been a wall, on the right side and on the left, while the people of Israel passed the sea dry-foot. And with that rod he smote the rock, and the water came out of it; and with that rod he did many other wonders.

And therein was a vessel of gold, full of manna, and clothings, and ornaments, and the tabernacle of Aaron, and a square tabernacle of gold, with twelve precious stones, and a box of green jasper, with four figures, and eight names of our Lord, and seven candlesticks of gold, and twelve pots of gold, and four censers of gold, and an altar of gold, and four lions of gold, which bare cherubim of gold twelve spans long, and the circle of swans of heaven, with a tabernacle of gold, and a table of silver, and two trumpets of silver, and seven barley loaves, and all the other relics that were before the birth of our Lord Jesus Christ.

And Jacob was sleeping upon that rock when he saw the angels go up and down by a ladder, and he said, " Surely the Lord is in this place; and I knew it not." And there an angel held Jacob still, and changed his name, and called him Israel. And in that same place David saw the angel that smote the people with a sword, and put it up bloody in the sheath. And St. Simeon was on that same rock when he received our Lord into the temple. And in this rock he placed himself when the Jews would have stoned him; and a star came down and gave him light. On that rock our Lord preached frequently to the people, and out of that same temple our Lord drove the buyers and sellers. Upon that rock also our Lord sat Him when the Jews would have stoned Him; and the rock clave in two, and in that cleft was our Lord hid; and there came down a star and gave Him light; and upon that rock our Lady sat and learned her Psalter; and there our Lord forgave the woman her sins that was found in adultery; and there our Lord was circumcised; and there the angel gave tidings to Zacharias of the birth of St. John the Baptist, his son; and there first Melchizedek offered bread and wine to our Lord, in token of the sacrament that was to come; and there David fell down praying to our Lord, and to the angel that smote the people, that He would have mercy on him and on the people; and our Lord heard his prayer, and therefore would He make the temple in that place; but our Lord forbade him, by an angel, because he had done treason when he caused Uriah, the worthy knight, to be slain, to have Bathsheba, his wife; and therefore all the materials he had collected for the building of the temple he gave to Solomon, his son, and he built it.

Without the gate of that temple is an altar, where the Jews were wont to offer doves and turtles. And between the temple and that altar was Zacharias slain. Upon the pinnacle of that temple was our Lord brought to be tempted by the fiend. And on the top of that pinnacle the Jews placed St. James, who was first bishop of Jerusalem, and cast him down to the earth. At the entry of the temple, toward the west, is the gate that is called the Beautiful Gate. And near the temple, on the right, is a church covered with lead, called Solomon's school. And near the temple, on the south, is the temple of Solomon, which is very fair and well polished. And in that temple dwelt the knights of the temple, that were called Templars; and that was the foundation of their order; so that knights dwelt there, and canons regular, in the temple of our Lord.

One hundred and twenty paces from that temple to the east, in the corner of the city, is the bath of our Lord; and in that bath water was wont to come from Paradise, and still it droppeth. And there beside is our Lady's bed. And fast by is the temple of St. Simeon; and without the cloister of the temple, toward the north, is a very fair church of St. Anne, our Lady's mother; and there our Lady was conceived. And before that church is a great tree, which began to grow the same night. And under that church, in going down by twenty-two steps, lies Joachim, our Lady's father, in a fair tomb of stone; and there beside lay sometime St. Anne, his wife; but St. Helena caused her to be translated to Constantinople. And in that church is a well, in manner of a cistern, which is called *Probatica Piscina*, which hath five entrances. Angels used to come from heaven into that well and bathe them in it, and the man who first bathed after the moving of the water, was made whole of whatever sickness he had; and there our Lord healed a man of the palsy, with which he had lain thirty-eight years; and our Lord said to him, "Take up thy bed and go."

And near it was Pilate's house. And fast by is King Herod's

house, who caused the Innocents to be slain. This Herod was excessively wicked and cruel; for first he caused his wife to be killed, whom he loved well; and for the great love he had to her, when he saw her dead, he fell in a rage, and was out of his mind a great while; and after he recovered, he caused his two sons, whom he had by that wife, to be slain; and after that he killed another of his wives, and a son that he had by her; and after that he put to death his own mother, and he would have slain his brother also, but he died suddenly. And after he fell into sickness, and when he felt that he should die, he sent for his sister and for all the lords of his land, and he sent them to prison; and then he said to his sister, he knew well that people would make no sorrow for his death, and therefore he made his sister swear that she should cause all the heads of the lords to be struck off when he was dead, that all the land might make sorrow for his death. But his sister fulfilled not his will; for as soon as he was dead she delivered all the lords out of prison, and told them all the purpose of her brother's ordinance; and so this cursed king was never made sorrow for. And you must know that at that time there were three Herods, of great fame for their cruelty. This Herod of which I have spoken was Herod the Ascalonite: and he that caused St. John the Baptist to be beheaded was Herod Antipas; and he that caused St. James to be beheaded was Herod Agrippa; and he put St. Peter in prison.

Furthermore, in the city is the Church of St. Saviour, where is preserved the left arm of John Chrysostom, and the greater part of the head of St. Stephen. On the other side of the street, to the south, as men go to Mount Sion, is a church of St. James, where he was beheaded. And one hundred and twenty paces from that church is Mount Sion, where there is a fair church of our Lady, where she dwelt and died. And there was formerly an abbot of canons regular. From thence she was carried by the apostles to the valley of Jehoshaphat, and there is the stone which the angel brought to our Lady from Mount Sinai, which is of the same color as the rock of St. Catharine. And near there is the gate through which our Lady passed, when she was with child, on her way to Bethelehem. Also, at the entrance of Mount Sion is a chapel in which is the great stone with which the sepulcher was covered, when Joseph of Arimathea had put our Lord therein; which stone the three Marys saw turned upward when they came to His sepulcher the day of His resurrection; and there they found an angel, who told them of our Lord's resurrection from death to life.

There also, in a wall beside the gate, is a stone of the pillar at which our Lord was scourged, and there was the house of Annas, who was bishop of the Jews at that time; and there our Lord was examined in the night, and scourged, and smitten, and violently treated. In that same place St. Peter forsook our Lord thrice before the cock crew. There is a part of the table on which He made His Supper, when He made His Maundy with His disciples, and gave them His flesh and His blood, in form of bread and wine. And under that chapel by a descent of thirty-two steps, is the place where our Lord washed His disciples' feet, and the vessel which contained the water is still preserved; and there, beside that same vessel, was St. Stephen buried. And there is the altar where our Lord heard the angels sing Mass. And there our Lord appeared first to His disciples after His resurrection, the doors being shut, and said to them, "Peace to you!" And on that Mount Christ appeared to St. Thomas the Apostle, and bade him feel His wounds; and there he first believed, and said, "My Lord and my God." In the same church, beside the altar, were all the apostles on Whitsunday, when the Holy Ghost descended on them in likeness of fire.

Mount Sion is within the city, and is a little higher than the other side of the city; and the city is strongest on that side. For at the foot of Mount Sion is a fair and strong castle made by the sultan. In Mount Sion were buried King David and King Solomon, and many other Jewish kings of Jerusalem. And there is the place where the Jews would have cast up the body of our Lady, when the apostles carried the body to be buried in the Valley of Jehoshaphat. And there is the place where St. Peter wept bitterly after he had forsaken our Lord. And a stone's cast from that chapel is another chapel, where our Lord was judged; for at that time the house of Caiaphas stood there.

One hundred and forty paces from that chapel, to the east, is a deep cave under the rock, which is called the Galilee of our Lord, where St. Peter hid himself when he had forsaken our Lord. Between Mount Sion and the Temple of Solomon is the place where our Lord raised the maiden in her father's house. Under Mount Sion, toward the Valley of Jehoshaphat, is a well called Natatorium Siloæ (the pool of Siloah), where our Lord was washed after His baptism; and there our Lord made the blind man to see. There was buried Isaiah the prophet. Also straight from Natatorium Siloæ is an image of stone, and of ancient work, which Absalom caused to be made, on account of which they call it the hand of Absalom.

And fast by is still the elder tree on which Judas hanged himself for despair, when he sold and betrayed our Lord. Near it was the synagogue, where the bishops of the Jews and the Pharisees came together and held their council, and where Judas cast the thirty pence before them, and said that he had sinned in betraying our Lord. And near it was the house of the apostles Philip and James the son of Alpheus. On the other side of Mount Sion, toward the south, a stone's cast beyond the vale, is Aceldama, that is, the field of blood, which was bought for the thirty pence for which our Lord was sold; in which field are many tombs of Christians; for there are many pilgrims' graves. And there are many oratories, chapels, and hermitages, where hermits used to dwell. A hundred paces toward the east is the charnel-house of the Hospital of St. John, where they used to put the bones of dead men.

To the west of Jerusalem is a fair church, where the tree of the cross grew. And two miles from thence is a handsome church, where our Lady met with Elizabeth, when they were both with child; and St. John stirred in his mother's womb, and made reverence to his Creator, whom he saw not. Under the altar of that church is the place where St. John was born. A mile from that church is the castle of Emmaus, where our Lord showed Himself to two of His disciples after His resurrection. Also on the other side, two hundred paces from Jerusalem, is a church, where was formerly the cave of the lion; and under that church, at thirty steps deep, were interred twelve thousand martyrs, in the time of King Cosrhoes, that the lion met in a night, by the will of God.

Two miles from Jerusalem is Mount Joy, a very fair and delicious place. There Samuel the prophet lies, in a fair tomb; and it is called Mount Joy, because it gives joy to pilgrims' hearts, for from that place men first see Jerusalem. Between Jerusalem and Mount Olivet is the Valley of Jehoshaphat, under the walls of the city as I have said before; and in the middle of the valley is a little river, which is called the brook Cedron; and across it lies a tree (of which the cross was made), on which men passed over; and fast by it is a little pit in the earth, where the foot of the pillar still remains at which our Lord was first scourged; for He was scourged and shamefully treated in many places.

Also in the middle of the Valley of Jehoshaphat is the Church of our Lady, which is forty-three steps below the sepulcher of our Lady, who was seventy-two years of age when she died. Beside the sepulcher of our Lady is an altar, where our Lord forgave St. Peter all his sins. From thence, toward the west, under an altar, is a well which comes out of the river of Paradise. You must know that that church is very low in the earth, and a part is quite within the earth. But I imagine that it was not founded so; but since Jerusalem has often been destroyed, and the walls beaten down and tumbled into the valley, and that they have been so filled again, and the ground raised, for that reason the church is so low within the earth. Nevertheless, men say there commonly, that the earth hath so been cloven since the time that our Lady was buried there; and men also say there, that it grows and increases every day, without doubt.

In that church were formerly black monks, who had their abbot. Beside that church is a chapel, beside the rock called Gethsemane, where our Lord was kissed by Judas, and where He was taken by the Jews; and there our Lord left His disciples when He went to pray before His passion, when He prayed and said, "O My Father, if it be possible, let this cup pass from Me." And when He came again to His disciples, He found them sleeping. And in the rock within the chapel we still see the mark of the fingers of our Lord's hand, when He put them on the rock when the Jews would have taken Him. And a stone's cast from thence, to the south, is another chapel, where our Lord sweat drops of blood. And close to it is the tomb of King Jehoshaphat, from whom the valley takes its name. This Jehoshaphat was king of that country, and was converted by a hermit, who was a worthy man, and did much-good.

A bow-shot from thence, to the south, is the church where St. James and Zachariah the prophet were buried. Above the vale is Mount Olivet, so called for the abundance of olives that grow there. That mount is higher than the city of Jerusalem; and therefore from that mount we may see many of the streets of the city. Between that mount and the city is only the Valley of Jehoshaphat, which is not wide. From that mount our Lord Jesus Christ ascended to heaven on Ascension-day, and yet there appears the imprint of His left foot in the stone. And there is a church where were formerly an abbot, and canons regular.

About twenty-eight paces thence is a chapel, in which is the stone on the which our Lord sat when He preached the eight blessings And there He taught His disciples the Pater Noster, and wrote with His finger on a stone. And near it is a church of St Mary, the Egyptian, where she lies in a tomb. Three bow-shots thence, to the east, is Bethphage, whither our Lord sent St. Peter and St. James on Palm Sunday to seek the ass on which he rode into Jerusalem. In descending from Mount Olivet, to the east, is a castle called Bethany, where dwelt Simon the Leper; and there he entertained our Lord; afterward he was baptized by the apostles, and was called Julian, and was made bishop, and this is the same Julian to whom men pray for good entertainment, because our Lord was entertained by him in his house. In that house our Lord forgave Mary Magdalene her sins, and there she washed His feet with her tears, and wiped them with her hair. And there St. Martha waited upon our Lord. There our Lord raised Lazarus, who was dead four days and stunk. There also dwelt Mary Cleophas. That castle is a mile from Jerusalem.

Also in coming down from Mount Olivet is the place where our Lord wept upon Jerusalem. And there beside is the place where our Lady appeared to St. Thomas the Apostle after her assumption, and gave him her girdle. And very near it is the stone on which our Lord often sat when He preached; and upon that same shall He sit at the day of doom, right as He said Himself.

After Mount Olivet is the Mount of Galilee, where the apostles assembled when Mary Magdalene came and told them of Christ's ascension. And there, between Mount Olivet and the Mount of Galilee, is a church, where the angel foretold our Lady of her death. We next go from Bethany to Jericho, which was once a little city, but it is now destroyed, and is but a little village. Joshua took that city by miracle of God, and destroyed it and cursed it, and all them that should build it again. Of that city was Zaccheus the dwarf, who climbed up into the sycamore-tree to see our Lord, because he was so little he might not see Him for the people. And of that city was Rahab, the harlot, who alone escaped with her kinspeople; and she often refreshed and fed the messengers of Israel, and kept them from many great perils of death; and therefore she had good reward; as Holy Writ saith, "He that receiveth a prophet in the name of a prophet, shall receive a prophet's reward;" and so had she: for she prophesied to the messengers, saying, "I know that the Lord hath given you the land;" and so He did.

From Bethany you go to the River Jordan, by a mountain, and through a desert; and it is nearly a day's journey from Bethany, toward the east, to a great hill, where our Lord fasted forty days. The devil carried our Lord upon that hill, and tempted Him, and said, "Command that these stones be made bread." In that place, upon the hill, there was formerly a fair church, but it is entirely destroyed, so that there is now but a hermitage, occupied by a kind of Christians called Georgians, because St. George converted them. Upon that hill dwelt Abraham a long while; and therefore they call it Abraham's garden. Between the hill and this garden runs a little brook of water, which was formerly bitter, but, when blessed by the Prophet Elisha, it became sweet and good to drink. At the foot of this hill toward the plain is a great well, which flows into the River Jordan. From that hill to Jericho is but a mile, in going toward the River Jordan, which is two miles beyond it; and half a mile nearer is a fair church of St. John the Baptist, where he baptized our Lord; and there beside is the house of Jeremiah the prophet.

CHAPTER IX.

OF THE DEAD SEA, AND OF THE RIVER JORDAN—OF THE HEAD OF ST. JOHN THE BAPTIST, AND OF THE USAGES OF THE SAMARITANS.

From Jericho it is three miles to the Dead Sea. About that sea groweth much alum and alkatran. Between Jericho and that sea is the land of Dengadda, where formerly balm grew; but men caused the branches to be drawn up and carried to Babylon, and still they call them vines of Gady. On the coast of that sea, as we go from Arabia, is the Mount of the Moabites, where there is a cave which they call Karua. Upon that hill Balak, the son of Boaz, led Balaam the priest to curse the people of Israel. The Dead Sea divides the lands of India and Arabia, and the sea reaches from Soara to Arabia

The water of that sea is very bitter and salt, and if the earth were moistened with that water it would never bear fruit. And the earth and land change often their color. The water casteth out a thing that is called asphalt, in pieces as large as a horse, every day and on all sides. From Jerusalem to that sea is two hundred furlongs. That sea is in length five hundred and eighty furlongs, and in breadth one hundred and fifty furlongs, and is called the Dead Sea, because it does not run, but is ever motionless. Neither man, beast, or anything that hath life, may die in that sea; and that hath been proved many times by men that have been condemned to death, who have been cast therein, and left therein three or four days, and they might never die therein, for it receiveth nothing within him that breatheth life. And no man may drink of the water on account of its bitterness. And if a man cast iron therein, it will float on the surface; but if men cast a feather therein, it will sink to the bottom; and these are things contrary to nature. And there beside grow trees that bear apples very fair of color to behold; but when we break or cut them in two we find within ashes and cinders, which is a token that by the wrath of God the cities and the land were burned and sunk into hell. Some call that sea the Lake Dasfetidee; some, the River of Devils; and some, the river that is ever stinking.

Into that sea, by the wrath of God, sunk the five cities, Sodom, Gomorrah, Aldama, Seboym, and Segor, for the abominable sin that reigned in them. But Segor, by the prayer of Lot, was saved and kept a great while, for it was set upon a hill, and some part of it still appears above the water; and men may see the walls when it is fair and clear weather. In that city Lot dwelt a little while; and there was he made drunk by his daughters, and lay with them, and begat on them Moab and Amon. The hill above Segor was then called Edom, but afterward men called it Seyr, and subsequently Idumea. At the right side of the Dead Sea the wife of Lot still stands in likeness of a salt stone, because she looked behind her when the cities sunk into hell.

And you shall understand that the River Jordan runs into the Dead Sea, and there it dies, for it runs no further; and its entrance is a mile from the Church of St. John the Baptist, toward the west, a little beneath the place where Christians bathe commonly. A mile from the River Jordan is the River of Jabbok, which Jacob passed over when he came from Mesopotamia. This River Jordan is no great river, but it has plenty of good fish; and it cometh out of the hill of Libanus by two wells, that are called Jor and Dan; and of those two wells it hath its name. It passes by a lake called Maron; and after, it passes through the Sea of Tiberias and under the hills of Gilboa; and there is a very fair valley on both sides of the river.

The hills of Libanus reach in length to the desert of Pharan. And these hills separate the Kingdom of Syria and the country of Phœnicia. Upon these hills grow cedar trees, that are very high, and bear long apples, as great as a man's head. This River Jordan also separates the land of Galilee and the land of Idumea, and the land of Betron; and it runs under the earth a great way, unto a fair and great plain, which is called Meldan, in the language of Sarmoyz; that is to say, a fair or market, in their language, because fairs are often held in that plain. And there becomes the water great and wide. That plain is the tomb of Job. About the river Jordan are many churches, where many Christian men dwelt. And near it is the city of Hay, which Joshua assailed and took. Also beyond the River Jordan is the Valley of Mamre, and that is a very fair valley. Also upon the hill that I spoke of before, where

our Lord fasted forty days, two miles from Galilee, is a fair and
lofty hill, where the fiend carried our Lord, the third time, to tempt
Him, and showed Him all the regions of the world, and said, "All
this shall I give Thee if Thou fall down and worship me."

In going eastward from the Dead Sea, out of the borders of the
Holy Land, is a strong and fair castle, on a hill which is called
Carak, in Sarmoyz; that is to say, Royal. That castle was made
by King Baldwin, when he had conquered that land, who put it into
the hands of Christians, to keep that part of the country; and for
that cause it was called the Mount Royal; and under it there is a
town called Sobache; and there all about dwell Christians, under
tribute. From thence men go to Nazareth, of which our Lord
beareth the surname. And thence it is three days to Jerusalem; and
men go by the province of Galilee, by Ramoth, by Sodom, and by
the high hill of Ephraim, where Elkanah and Hannah, the mother
of Samuel the prophet, dwelt. There this prophet was born;
and, after his death, he was buried at Mount Joy, as I have said before. And then men go to Shiloh, where the ark of God with the
relics were long kept under Eli the prophet.

There the people of Hebron sacrificed to our Lord; and there they
yielded up their vows; and there God first spake to Samuel, and
showed him the change of the order of priesthood, and the mystery
of the sacrament. And right nigh, on the left side, is Gibeon, and
Ramah, and Benjamin, of which Holy Writ speaketh. And after
men go to Shechem, formerly called Sicher, which is in the province
of the Samaritans; and there is a very fair and fruitful vale, and
there is a fair and good city, called Neapolis, whence it is a day's
journey to Jerusalem. And there is the well where our Lord spake
to the woman of Samaria; and there was wont to be a church, but
it is beaten down. Beside that well King Rehoboam caused two
calves to be made of gold, and made them to be worshiped, and put
the one at Dan and the other at Bethel.

A mile from Sichar is the city of Deluze, in which Abraham
dwelt a certain time. Shechem is ten miles from Jerusalem, and
is called Neapolis, that is to say, the new city. And near it is the
tomb of Joseph, the son of Jacob, who governed Egypt; for the
Jews carried his bones from Egypt, and buried them there; and
thither the Jews go oftentime in pilgrimage, with great devotion. In
that city was Dinah, Jacob's daughter, ravished; for which her
brethren slew many persons, and did many injuries to the city. And
there beside is the hill of Gerizim, where the Samaritans make their
sacrifice; on that hill would Abraham have sacrificed his son Isaac.

And there beside is the Valley of Dothan; and there is the cistern wherein Joseph was cast by his brethren, when they sold him; and that is two miles from Sichar.

From thence we go to Samaria, which is now called Sebaste; it is the chief city of that country, and is situated between the hill of Aygnes in a similar manner to Jerusalem. In that city were the sittings of the twelve tribes of Israel; but the city is not now so great as it was formerly. There St. John the Baptist was buried, between two prophets, Elisha and Abdias; but he was beheaded in the castle of Macharyme, near the Dead Sea; and after he was carried by his disciples, and buried at Samaria; and there Julian the Apostate caused him to be dug up, and burned his bones, and cast his ashes to the wind. But the finger that showed our Lord, saying, "Behold the Lamb of God!" would never burn, but is all whole; St. Tecla, the holy virgin, caused that finger to be carried to the hill of Sebaste, and there men made great feast for it.

In that place was wont to be a fair church; and many others there were, but they are all beaten down. There was wont to be the head of St. John the Baptist, inclosed in the wall; but the Emperor Theodosius had it drawn out, and found it wrapped in a little cloth, all bloody; and so he carried it to Constantinople: and the hinder part of the head is still at Constantinople; and the fore part of the head, to under the chin, is at Rome, under the Church of St. Silvester, where are nuns; and it is yet all broiled, as though it were half burned; for the Emperor Julian above mentioned, of his wickedness and malice, burned that part with the other bones, as may still be seen; and this thing hath been proved both by popes and emperors. And the jaws beneath, which hold to the chin, and a part of the ashes, and the platter on which the head was laid when it was smitten off, are at Genoa; and the Genoese make a great feast in honor of it, and so do the Saracens also. And some men say that the head of St. John is at Amiens, in Picardy; and other men say, that it is the head of St. John the bishop. I know not which is correct, but God knows; but however men worship it, the blessed St. John is satisfied.

From this city of Sebaste unto Jerusalem it is twelve miles. And between the hills of that country there is a well that four times in the year changes its color; sometimes green, sometimes red, sometimes clear, and sometimes troubled; and men call that well Job. And the people of that country, who are called Samaritans, were converted and baptized by the Apostles, but they hold not well their doctrine; and always they hold laws by themselves, varying from Christian men, from Saracens, Jews, and Pagans. The Samaritans believe well in one God; and they say there is only one God, who created all things, and judges all things; and they hold the Bible according to the letter, and use the Psalter as the Jews do: and they say that they are the right sons of God; and, among all other folk, they say that they be best beloved of God, and that to them belongs the heritage that God promised to his beloved children; and they have also a different clothing and outward appearance from other people, for they wrap their heads in red linen cloth, as a distinction from others; and the Saracens wrap their heads in white linen cloth: and the Christian men that dwell in the country wrap them in blue of India and the Jews in yellow cloth. In that country dwell many of the Jews paying tribute as Christians do.

CHAPTER X.

OF THE PROVINCE OF GALILEE, AND WHERE ANTICHRIST SHALL BE BORN—OF NAZRETH—OF THE AGE OF OUR LADY—OF THE DAY OF DOOM; AND OF THE CUSTOMS OF JACOBITES, SYRIANS, AND GEORGIANS.

FROM this country of the Samaritans men go to the plains of Galilee and leave the hills, on the one side. Galilee is one of the provinces of the Holy Land: and in that province are the cities of Nain, and Capernaum and Chorazin, and Bethsaida. In this Bethsaida St. Peter and St. Andrew were born. And four miles thence is Chorazin: and five miles from Chorazin is the city of Kedar, whereof the Psalter speaketh: "I dwell in the tents of Kedar." In Chorazin shall Antichrist be born, as some men say; and others say he shall be born in Babylon; for the prophet saith, "Out of Babylon shall come a serpent that shall devour all the world." This Antichrist shall be nourished in Bethsaida, and he shall reign in Capernaum: and therefore saith Holy Writ, "Woe unto thee, Chorazin! woe unto thee, Bethsaida! and thou, Capernaum." And all these towns are in the land of Galilee; and also Cana of Galilee is four miles from Nazareth, of which city was Simon the Canaanite and his wife Cance, of whom the holy Evangelist speaks; there our Lord performed the first miracle at the wedding, when He turned water into wine.

And at the extremity of Galilee, on the hills, was the ark of God taken; and on the other side is Mount Hendor, or Hermon. And thereabout goeth the brook of Kishon; and near there Baruch, who was son of Abimelech, with Deborah the prophetess, overcame the host of Idumea, when Sisera the king was slain by Jael, the wife of Heber, and Gideon drove beyond the River Jordan, by strength of the sword, Zeba and Zalmunna, and there he slew them. Also five miles from Nain is the city of Jezreel, which was formerly called Zarim, of which city Jezabel the wicked queen was lady and queen, who took away the vineyard of Naboth by force. Fast by that city is the field Magedo, in which King Joras was slain by the king of Samaria, and after was carried and buried in Mount Sion. A mile from Jezreel are the hills of Gilboa, where Saul and Jonathan, that were so fair, died; and wherefore David cursed them, as Holy Writ saith: "Ye mountains of Gilboa, let there be no dew, neither let there be rain, upon you." A mile from the hills of Gilboa, to the east, is the city of Cyropolis, which was before called Bethsain; and upon the walls of that city was the head of Saul hanged.

After men go by the hills, beside the plains of Galilee, unto Nazareth, which was formerly a great and fair city, but now there is but a small village, and houses scattered here and there. It is not walled, but it is situated in a little valley, with hills all about. Here our Lady was born; but she was begotten at Jerusalem; and because our Lady was born at Nazareth, therefore our Lord bare His surname of that town. There Joseph took our Lady to wife, when she was fourteen years of age; and there Gabriel greeted our Lady, saying, "Hail, thou that art highly favored, the Lord is with thee." And this salutation was made on the site of a great altar of a fair church that stood there formerly, but it is now all down; and they have made a little receptacle, near a pillar of that church, to receive the offerings of pilgrims. And the Saracens keep that place full dearly, for the profit they have by it; and they are very wicked and cruel Saracens, and more spiteful than in any other place, and have destroyed all the churches.

Near there is Gabriel's well, where our Lord was wont to bathe, when He was young; and from that well He carried water often to His mother; and in that well she often washed the clothes of her son Jesus Christ; and from Jerusalem thither is three days. Two miles from Nazareth is the city of Sephor, by the way that goes from Nazareth to Acre. And half a mile from Nazareth is the leap of our Lord; for the Jews led Him upon a high rock, to make Him leap down, and have slain Him; but Jesus passed amongst them, and leaped upon another rock; and the steps of His feet are still to be seen in the rock where He alighted. And therefore men say, when in traveling they are in fear of thieves or enemies, "*Jesus autem transiens per medium illorum ibat;*" that is to say, "But Jesus, passing through the midst of them, went:" in token and remembrance, that as our Lord passed through the Jews' cruelty, and escaped safely from them, so surely may men escape the peril of thieves; and then men say two verses of the Psalter three times: "*Irruat super eos formido et pavor, in magnitudine brachii tui, Domine; fiant inmobiles, quasi lapis, donec pertranseat populus tuus, Domine; donec pertranseat populus tuus iste, quem possedisti.*" ('May fear and dread fall upon them; by the greatness of Thine arm, O Lord! let them be as still as a stone; till thy people pass over, O Lord! till the people pass over, which thou hast purchased.") And then men may pass without peril. And you shall understand, that our Lady had child when she was fifteen years old; and she was conversant with her son thirty-three years and three months. And after the passion of our Lord she lived twenty-four years.

From Nazareth we go four miles to Mount Tabor, which is a very fair and lofty hill, where were formerly a town and many churches, but they are all destroyed; but yet there is a place, which they call the School of God, where he was wont to teach His disciples, and told them the secrets of Heaven. At the foot of that hill Melchizedek, who was King of Salem, met Abraham in the turning of the hill on his return from the battle, when he had slain Abimelech; and this Melchizedek was both king and priest of Salem, which is now called Jerusalem. On that hill of Tabor our Lord transfigured Himself before St. Peter, St. John, and St. James; and there they saw in spirit Moses and Elias the prophets, and therefore St. Peter said, "Lord, it is good for us to be here; let us make here three tabernacles."

On that hill and in that same place, at Doomsday, four angels shall blow with four trumpets, and raise all men that have suffered death since the world was created to life; and they shall come in body and soul in judgment, before the face of our Lord, in the Valley of Jehoshaphat. And it shall be on Easter-day, the time of our Lord's resurrection; and the judgment shall begin on the same hour that our Lord descended to hell and despoiled it; for at that hour shall He despoil the world, and lead His chosen to bliss; and the others shall be condemned to perpetual punishment; and then shall every man have after his desert, either good or evil, unless the mercy of God exceed His righteousness.

A mile from Mount Tabor is Mount Hermon, and there was the city of Nain. Before the gate of that city our Lord raised the widow's son. Three miles from Nazareth is the Castle of Saffra, of which were the sons of Zebedee and the sons of Alpheus. Also, seven miles from Nazareth, is Mount Cain, under which is a well, and beside that well, Lamech, Noah's father, slew Cain with an arrow. For this Cain went through briers and bushes as a wild beast; and he had lived from the time of Adam, his father, unto the time of Noah; and so he lived nearly two thousand years. And Lamech was blind for old age.

From Saffra we go to the Sea of Galilee, and to the city of Tiberias, which is situated upon that sea. And although they call it a sea, it is neither sea, nor arm of the sea; for it is but a stank of fresh water, which is in length one hundred furlongs, and in breadth forty furlongs; and it hath in it great plenty of good fish, and the River Jordan runs through it. The city is not very great, but it has good baths. And where the River Jordan leaves the Sea of Galilee is a great bridge, where they pass from the land of Promise to the land of Bashan and the land of Gerrasentz, which are about the River Jordan and the commencement of the Sea of Tiberias.

And from thence may men go to Damascus in three days, by the kingdom of Traconitis, which kingdom extends from Mount Hermon to the Sea of Galilee, or the Sea of Tiberias, or the Sea of Genesareth, which are different names of this sea, or rather this stank, of which I have spoken, which changes thus its name according to the names of the cities that are situated beside it. On that sea our Lord went dry-foot; and there He took up St. Peter, when he began to sink in the sea, and said to him, "O thou of little faith, wherefore didst thou doubt?" And after His resurrection our Lord appeared on that sea to His disciples, and bade them fish, and filled the net full of great fishes. In that sea our Lord rowed oftentime; and there He called to Him St. Peter, St. Andrew, and St. James, and St. John, the sons of Zebedee. In that city of Tiberias is the table on which our Lord eat with His disciples after His resurrection; and they knew Him in breaking of bread, as the Gospel saith.

And near the city of Tiberias is the hill where our Lord fed five thousand persons, with five barley loaves and two fishes. In that city a man cast a burning dart in wrath after our Lord, and the head smote into the earth, and waxed green, and it grew to a great tree; and it grows still, and the bark thereof is all like coals. Also in the head of that Sea of Galilee, toward the north, is a strong and lofty castle, called Saphor; and close by it is Capernaum; there is not so strong a castle within the land of Promise; and there is a good town beneath, also called Saphor. In that castle St. Anne, our Lady's mother, was born. And there, beneath, was the centurion's house.

That country is called the Galilee of the Gentiles, who were taken to tribute of Zebulon and Naphthali. And in returning from that castle, at a distance of thirty miles, is the city of Dan, formerly called Belinas, or Cesarea Philippi, situated at the foot of the mountain of Libanus, where the River Jordan arises. There begins the land of Promise, and it extends unto Beersheba, in length from north to south, and contains full one hundred and eighty miles; and in breadth, that is, from Jericho to Jaffa, it contains forty miles of Lombardy, or of our country, which are also little miles. These are not miles of Gascony, or of Germany, where the miles are great miles.

And you must know that the land of Promise is in Syria. For the realm of Syria extends from the deserts of Arabia to Cilicia, which is Armenia the Great, that is to say, from south to north; and from east to west it extends from the great deserts of Arabia to the west sea. But in that realm of Syria is the kingdom of Judea, and many other provinces, as Palestine, Galilee, Little Cilicia, and many others.

In that country, and other countries beyond, they have a custom, when they make war, and when men besiege a city or castle, and they within dare not send out messengers with letters from lord to lord to ask succor, of binding their letters to the necks of pigeons, and letting them fly; and the pigeons are so taught that they fly with those letters to the very place that men would send them to. For they are fed in those places where they are sent to, and they naturally return to where they have been fed.

And you shall understand that amongst the Saracens, in different parts, dwell many Christian men, of many kinds and different names, and all are baptized, and have different laws and different customs; but all believe in God the Father, and the Son, and the Holy Ghost; but they always fail in some articles of our faith. Some of these are called Jacobites, because St. James converted them, and St. John baptized them. They say that a man shall make his confession only to God, and not to a man; for only to Him should man acknowledge himself guilty of all that he hath misdone; and God ordained not, nor ever devised, nor the prophet either, that one man should confess himself to another (as they say), but only to God; as Moses writeth in the Bible, and as David saith in the Psalter Book, "I will confess to thee, O Lord, in my whole heart:" and "I acknowledge my sin unto thee:" and "Thou art my God, and

I will confess to thee:" and " Since the thoughts of man shall confess to thee," etc.

For they know all the Bible and the Psalter, and therefore allege they so the letter; but they allege not the authorities thus in Latin, but in their language full openly; and say well, that David and other prophets say it. Nevertheless St. Austin, St. Gregory, and St. Hilary say differently. And on such authorities, they say, that only to God shall a man confess his faults, acknowledging himself guilty, and crying Him mercy, and promising Him to amend; therefore when they will confess them, they take fire, and set it beside them, and cast therein powder of frankincense, and in the smoke thereof they confess them to God, and cry Him mercy. And true it is, that this confession was first and of nature; but St. Peter the Apostle, and they that came after him, have ordered to make confession to man; and by good reason, for they perceived well, that no sickness was curable by good medicine laid thereto, unless men knew the nature of the malady; and also no man may give fit medicine, unless he know the quality of the deed.

There are others who are called Syrians, who hold the belief among us and the Greeks; and they all use beards, as men of Greece do; and they make the sacrament of unleavened bread; and in their language they use the Saracenic letters, but in their theological mysteries they use Greek letters; and they make their confession as the Jacobites do.

There are others who are called Georgians, who were converted by St. George, and they worship him more than any other saint, and to him they cry for help; and they came out of the realm of Georgia. These people have their crowns shaven; the clerks have round crowns, and the laity have their crowns all square; and they hold the same Christian doctrines as the Greeks, of whom I have spoken before.

There are others who are called Christians of the girdle, because they are all girt above; and there are others called Nestorians; and some are Arians, some Nubians, some of Greece, some of India, and some of Prester John's land. And all these have many articles of our faith, and in others they differ from us.

CHAPTER XI.

OF THE CITY OF DAMASCUS—OF THREE WAYS TO JERUSALEM: ONE BY LAND AND BY SEA; ANOTHER MORE BY LAND THAN BY SEA; AND THE THIRD WAY TO JERUSALEM ALL BY LAND.

Now that I have told you of some of the people in the countries before, I will turn again to my way to describe the road back. From the land of Galilee, of which I have spoken, men come back to Damascus, which is a very fair and noble city, and full of all merchandise, and three days from the sea, and five days from Jerusalem. Men carry merchandise thither upon camels, mules, horses, dromedaries, and other beasts; and thither come merchants by sea, from India, Persia, Chaldea, Armenia, and many other kingdoms. This city was founded by Helizeus Damascus, who was yeoman and steward to Abraham before Isaac was born; for he expected to have been Abraham's heir, and he named the town after his surname, Damascus. And in that place, where Damascus was founded, Cain slew Abel his brother. And beside Damascus is Mount Seir.

In that city of Damascus there is great plenty of wells; and within the city and without are many fair gardens with diversity of fruits. No other city can be compared with it for fair gardens for recreation. The city is great and full of people, and well walled with double walls, and it contains many physicians; and St. Paul himself was there a physician, to keep men's bodies in health, before he was converted; and after that he was physician of souls. And St. Luke the Evangelist was a disciple of St. Paul to learn physic, and many others; for St. Paul held then a school of physic. And near Damascus he was converted; and after his conversion he dwelt in that city three days, without sight and without meat or drink. And in those three days he was raised to heaven, and there he saw many secrets of our Lord.

And close beside Damascus is the castle of Arkes, which is both fair and strong. From Damascus we return by our Lady of Sardenak, which is five miles on this side of Damascus; and it is seated upon a rock, and is a very fair place, and appears like a castle, which it was formerly; but it is now a very fair church; and in it are Christian monks and nuns; and there is a vault under the church where Christians dwell also; and they have many good vines. In the church, behind the altar, in the wall, is a table of black wood, on which formerly was painted an image of our Lady, which turns into flesh; but now the image appears but little. But evermore, through the grace of God, that table drops oil, as it were of olive. And there is a vessel of marble under the table, to receive the oil, of which they give to pilgrims; for it healeth many sicknesses. And he that keepeth it cleanly a year, after that year it turneth into flesh and blood.

Between the city of Dark and the city of Raphane is a river, which they call Sabatorye; for on the Saturday it runs fast, and all the week else it standeth still, and runs naught or little. And there is another river that freezeth wonderfully fast in the night, and by day no frost is seen. And so men go by a city called Beruthe, on the coast of the sea, by which they go to Cyprus; and they arrive at the port of Sur, or Tyre, and then to Cyprus. Or else men may go from the port of Tyre right well, and come not to Cyprus, but arrive at some haven of Greece; and then men come to this country by ways that I have spoken of before.

Now have I told you of ways by the which men go furthest and longest, as by Babylon and Mount Sinai, and many other places, through which lands men turn again to the land of Promise. Now I will tell you the direct way to Jerusalem; for some men will not pass it on account of the expense, or because they have no company, or for many other reasonable causes; and therefore I will tell you briefly how a man may go with little expense and in a short time.

A man who comes from the lands of the west, goes through France, Burgundy, and Lombardy, and to Venice, and to Genoa, or some other haven of the marshes, and taketh a ship there, and goes by sea to the Isle of Gryffle; and so he arrives in Greece, or in Port Moroche, or Valon, or Duras, or at some other haven, and lands to repose himself, and goes again to the sea, and arrives in Cyprus; and comes not to the Isle of Rhodes, but arrives at Famagosta, which is the chief haven of Cyprus, or else at Lamatoun, and then embarks again, and passes the haven of Tyre without landing; and so passes by all the havens of that coast till he comes to Jaffa, which is the nearest port to Jerusalem, for it is only seven-and-twenty miles.

And from Jaffa men go to the city of Ramla, which is but a short distance thence, and it is a fair city. And beside Ramla is a fair church of our Lady, where our Lord appeared to our Lady in the likeness that betokeneth the Trinity. And there, fast by, is a church of St George, where his head was smitten off; and then to the castle of Emmaus; and then to Mount Joy; and from thence pilgrims may first see Jerusalem. And then to Mount Modeyn, and then to Jerusalem. And at Mount Modeyn lies the Prophet Maccabeus. And over Ramatha is the town of Douke, whereof was Amos the good prophet.

Another way. Forasmuch as many men may not bear the sea, but had rather go by land, although it be a more laborious journey, a man shall so go to one of the havens of Lombardy, Venice, or another; and he shall pass into Greece, through Port Moroche or another, and so he shall go to Constantinople. And he shall so pass the water called the Brace of St. George, which is an arm of the sea; and from thence he shall come to Pulveralle, and thence to the castle of Cynople; and from thence he shall go to Cappadocia, which is a great country, where there are many great hills. And he shall go through Turkey, and unto the city of Nice, which the Turks have taken from the Emperor of Constantinople. It is a fair city, and wonderfully well walled: and there is a river that is called the Laye; and there men go by the Alps of Aryoprynant, and by the vales of Mallebrynez, and also the Vale of Ernax; and so to Antioch the Less, which is situated on the River Riclay. And thereabout are many good and fair hills, and many fair woods, and also wild beasts.

And he that will go by another way, must go by the plains of Romania, coasting the sea. Upon that coast is a wonderfully fair castle, which they call Florathe. And when we are out of those hills, we pass through a city called Maryoche and Arteyse, where there is a great bridge over the river of Ferne, which men call Farfar; and it is a great river, capable of admitting ships. And beside the city of Damascus is a river that comes from the Mountain of Libanus, which is called Albane. At the passing of this river St. Eustache lost his two sons, when he had lost his wife. And it goeth through the plain of Arthadoe, and so to the Red Sea; and so men go unto the city of Phenne, and so to the city of Ferne.

Antioch is a very fair city, and well walled; it is two miles long, and each pillar of the bridge there has a good tower; and this is the best city of the Kingdom of Syria. And from Antioch men may go to the city of Latuche (Latakiyah), and then to Gebel (Jebili), and then to Tourtous (Tortosa); and thereby is the land of Cambre, where there is a strong castle, which they call Maubeke. And from Tourtcus men go to Tripoli, on the sea; and they go by sea unto Acre. From this place there are two ways to Jerusalem; on the left we go first to Damas, by the River Jordan; on the right we go through the land of Flagam, and so to the city of Caiaphas (Caiffa), of which Caiaphas was lord; and some call it the Castle of Pilgrims. And from thence it is four days to Jerusalem, passing through Cesarea Philippi, Jaffa, Ramleh, and Emmaus.

Now I have told you some of the ways by land and water, how men may go to Jerusalem; but there are many other ways according to the countries from which they come. There is one way, all by land, to Jerusalem without passing any sea, which is from France or Flanders; but that way is very long and perilous, and therefore few go that way. It lies through Germany and Prussia, and so on to Tartary. This Tartary is held of the Great Chan, of whom I shall speak more afterward; and the lords of Tartary pay the Great Chan tribute. This is a very bad land, and sandy, and bears very little fruit; for there grows little corn, or wine, or beans, or pease; but there are plenty of cattle; and men eat nothing but flesh, without bread; and they drink the broth, and also they drink milk. And they eat all manner of animals, such as dogs, cats, and rats. And they have little or no wood; and therefore they warm and boil their meat with horse-dung, and cow-dung, and that of other beasts, dried by the sun; and princes and others eat but once a day, and that but little, and they are very foul people, and of evil nature.

And in summer, in all these countries, fall many tempests, and dreadful storms of thunder and lightning, which kill many people, and beasts also. And the temperature passes suddenly from extreme heat to extreme cold. It is the foulest country, and the most cursed, and the poorest, that men know. And their prince, whom they call Batho, dwells at the city of Orda. And truly no good man would dwell in that country; for it is not worthy for dogs to dwell in. It were a good country to sow thistles, and briers, and broom, and thorns; and it is good for no other thing. There is some good land, but very little, as men say. I have not been in that country; but I have been in other lands which border on those countries, and in the land of Russia, and in Nyflan, and in the realm of Cracow, and Letto (Lithuania), and in Darestan, and in many other places which border on those parts; but I never went by that way to Jerusalem, wherefore I can not describe it from personal knowledge; for no man may pass by that way well, except in time of winter, for the perilous waters and difficult marshes, which no man may pass except it be strong frost, and snow upon it; for if the snow were not there, men might not go upon the ice.

And it is full three days of such way to pass from Prussia to the inhabited land of the Saracens. And Christians who shall war against them every year must carry their victuals with them; for they shall find no good there. And they must carry their victual upon the ice, with cars that have no wheels, which they call sleighs; and as long as their victuals last they may abide there, but no longer; for there shall they find nobody that will sell them anything. And when the spies see any Christian men coming upon them, they run to the towns, and cry with a loud voice, "Kerra, kerra, kerra;" and then anon they arm and assemble together.

And you shall understand that it freezeth more strongly in those countries than in this part of the world; and therefore hath every man stoves in his house, and on those stoves they eat and do their occupations all that they may; for that is in the northern parts, where there is but little sun; and therefore in the very north the land is so cold that no man may dwell there; and, on the contrary, toward the south it is so hot that no man may dwell there, because there the sun is direct over head.

CHAPTER XII.

OF THE CUSTOMS OF THE SARACENS, AND OF THE LAW; AND HOW THE SULTAN DISCOURSED TO ME, THE AUTHOR OF THIS BOOK; AND OF MOHAMMED.

Now since I have spoken of Saracens and of their country, if you will know a part of their law and belief, I will tell you, according to their book, which is called Alkoran. And some call that book Meshaf; and some call it Harm, according to the different languages of the country. This book Mohammed gave them. In it, among other things, is written, as I have often seen and read, that the good shall go to Paradise, and the evil to hell; and that all Saracens believe. And if a man ask them what Paradise they mean, they say it is a place of delight, where men shall find all kinds of fruit, in all seasons, and rivers running with milk and honey, and wine and sweet water; and they shall have fair houses and noble, every man after his desert, made of precious stones, and of gold and silver; and every man shall have eighty wives.

Also they believe in and speak gladly of the Virgin Mary and of the Incarnation. And they say that Mary was taught of the angel; and that Gabriel said to her that she was chosen from the beginning of the world; and that he showed to her the incarnation of Jesus Christ; that she conceived, and bare a child, remaining a maid; and that witnesseth their book. And they say also that Jesus Christ spake as soon as He was born; and that He was a true and holy prophet in word and deed, and meek, and pious, and righteous, and without any vice. And they say also that when the angel showed the incarnation of Christ unto Mary, she was young, and had great fear. For there was then an enchanter in the country that dealt with witchcraft, called Taknia, who by his enchantments could take the likeness of an angel and went often and lay with maidens; and therefore Mary feared lest it had been Taknia, who came to deceive the maidens. And therefore she conjured the angel that he should tell her if it were he or no. And the angel answered and said that she should have no dread of him; for he was a true messenger of Jesus Christ.

Also their book says that when she had been delivered, under a palm-tree, she had great shame to have a child, and she moaned and said that she would that she had been dead. And anon the child spake to her and comforted her, and said, "Mother, have no fear, for God hath hid in thee His secrets, for the salvation of the world." And that book saith also that Jesus was sent from God Almighty to be a mirror and example to all men. And the Alkoran saith also, of the day of doom, how God shall come to judge all people; and the good He shall draw on His side and put them into bliss; and the wicked He shall condemn to the pains of hell. And they say that among all prophets Jesus was the most excellent and the most worthy, and that he made the Gospels, in which is good and healthful doctrine, full of charity and steadfastness, and true preaching to them that believe in God; and that He was a true prophet, and more than a prophet; and lived without sin, and gave sight to the blind, and healed the lepers, and raised dead men, and ascended to heaven. They fast a whole month in the year, eating only by night; and they keep from their wives all that month; but the sick are not bound to that fast.

Also this book speaks of the Jews, and says they are cursed, because they would not believe that Jesus Christ was come of God, and that they lied falsely on Mary and her son Jesus Christ, saying that they had crucified Jesus the son of Mary; for he was never crucified, as they say, but God made Him ascend to Him without death; but He transfigured His likeness into Judas Iscariot, and him the Jews crucified, believing that it had been Jesus; and therefore they say that the Christian men err, and have no good knowledge of this, and that they believe falsely that Jesus Christ was crucified. And they say also, that if He had been crucified, God had acted contrary to His righteousness, to suffer Jesus Christ, who was innocent, to be put upon the cross without guilt. And they say that we err in this article, and that the great righteousness of God might not suffer so great a wrong. They acknowledge that the works of Christ are good, and His words and His deeds and His doctrine by His Gospels true, and His miracles also true; and the blessed Virgin Mary was a good and holy maiden before and after the birth of Jesus Christ; and that all those that believe perfectly in God shall be saved. And because they go so nigh our faith, they are easily converted to Christian law, when men preach to them and show them distinctly the law of Jesus Christ, and tell them of the prophecies.

And also they say that they know well by the prophecies that the law of Mohammed shall fail as the law of the Jews did; and that the law of Christian people shall last to the day of doom. And if any man ask them what is their belief, they answer thus: "We believe in God, creator of heaven and earth, and all other things that He made. And without Him is nothing made.' . And we believe in the day of doom, and that every man shall have his merit according to his desert. And we hold for true all that God hath said by the mouths of His prophets." Also Mohammed commanded, in his Alkoran, that every man should have two wives, or three or four; but now they take as many as nine, and of lemans as many as a man may support. And if any one of their wives misbehave against her husband, he may cast her out of his house, and part from her and take another; but he shall share with her his goods.

Also when men speak to them of the Father and of the Son and of the Holy Ghost, they say that they be three persons, but not one God. For their Alkoran speaketh not of the Trinity. But they say well that God hath speech, and they know well God hath a spirit; for else, they say, he could not be alive. And when men speak to them of the incarnation, how by the word of the angel God sent His Wisdom into earth, and shadowed Him in the Virgin Mary; and by the word of God shall the dead be raised at the day of doom; they say that it is true, and that the word of God hath great power. And they say that whoso knew not the word of God, he should not know God. And they say also, that Jesus Christ is the word of God, and so saith their Alkoran, where it saith that the angel spake to Mary and said, "Mary, God shall preach the Gospel by the word of His mouth, and His name shall be called Jesus Christ."

And they say also that Abraham was friend to God, and that Moses spoke familiar with God; and Jesus Christ was the word and the spirit of God; and that Mohammed was the messenger of God.

And they say that of these four Jesus was the most worthy, and the most excellent and the greatest; so that they have many good articles of our faith, although they have no perfect law and faith as Christian men have, and therefore they are easily converted, especially those that understand the scriptures and the prophecies. For they have the Gospels, and the prophecies, and the Bible written in their language. Wherefore they know much of Holy Writ, but they understand it not but after the letter; and so do the Jews, for they understand not the letter spiritually, but carnally, and therefore be they reproved by the wise, who understand it spiritually.

The Saracens say that the Jews are cursed, because they have defiled the law that God sent them by Moses. And the Christians are cursed also, as they say, for they keep not the commandments and the precepts of the Gospel, which Jesus Christ gave them. And, therefore, I shall tell you what the sultan said to me one day, in his chamber. He sent out of his chamber all men, lords and others, because he would speak with me in counsel. And there he asked me how the Christian men governed themselves in our country?

And I answered, "Right well; thanked be God."

And he said to me, "Truly, nay; for you Christians care not how untruly you serve God. You should set an example to the common people to do well, and you set them an example of doing evil. For the commons, upon festival days, when they should go to church to serve God, go to taverns and are there in gluttony all day and night, and eat and drink as beasts that have no reason, and know not when they have enough. And also, the Christians encourage one another, in all ways that they may, to fight, and to deceive one another. And they are so proud that they know not how to be clothed; now long, now short, now straight, now large, now with sword, now with dagger, and in all manner of guises. They should be simple, meek, and true, and full of almsdeeds, as Jesus was, in whom they believe; but they are all the contrary, and ever inclined to evil, and to do evil. And they are so covetous, that for a little silver they sell their daughters, their sisters, and their own wives to put them to lechery. And one seduces the wife of another, and none of them holdeth faith to another; but they break their law, that Jesus Christ gave them to keep for their salvation. And thus, for their sins, have they lost all this land which we hold. Because, for their sins here, God hath given them into our hands; not only by our power, but for their sins. For we know well in very truth, that when you serve God, God will help you; and when He is with you, no man may be against you. And that know we well by our prophecies, that the Christians shall win again this land out of our hands when they serve God more devoutly. But as long as they are of foul and unclean living (as they are now), we have no dread of them, for their God will not help them."

And then I asked him how he knew the state of the Christians? And he answered me, "That he knew all the state of the commons also, by his messengers, whom he sent to all lands, in guise of merchants of precious stones, cloths of gold, and other things, to know the manners of every country amongst Christians."

And then he called in all the lords that he had sent out of his chamber, and he showed me four who were great lords, who told me of my country, and of many other Christian countries, as well as if they had been of the same country; and they spoke French perfectly well, and the sultan also, whereof I had great marvel. Alas! it is great slander to our faith and to our law, when people that are without law shall reprove us of our sins. And they that should be converted to Christ and to the law of Jesus by our good examples and by our acceptable life to God, and so converted to the law of Jesus Christ, are, through our wickedness and evil living, far from us, and strangers from the holy and true belief shall thus accuse us and hold us for wicked livers and accursed. And indeed they say truth. For the Saracens are good and faithful, and keep entirely the commandment of the holy book Alkoran, which God sent them by His messenger Mohammed; to whom, as they say, St. Gabriel the angel often told the will of God.

And you shall understand that Mohammed was born in Arabia, and was first a poor boy that kept camels which went with merchants for merchandise; and so it happened that he went with the merchants into Egypt. And in the deserts of Arabia he went into a chapel where a hermit dwelt; and when he entered into the chapel, which was but little and low, and had a small low door, then the entrance became so great, and so large, and so high as though it had been a great minster, or the gate of a palace. And this was the first miracle, the Saracens say, that Mohammed did in his youth.

Then he began to wax wise and rich; and he was a great astronomer; and afterward he was governor and prince of the land of Cozrodane, which he governed full wisely; in such manner that, when the prince was dead, he took his lady, named Gadrige, to wife. And Mohammed fell often in the great sickness called the falling evil, wherefore the lady was sorry that ever she took him to husband. But Mohammed made her believe that when he fell so Gabriel the angel came to speak with him, and for the great brightness of the angel he might not help falling. And therefore the Saracens say that Gabriel came often to speak with him.

This Mohammed reigned in Arabia in the year of our Lord Jesus Christ 610; and was of the generation of Ishmael; who was Abraham's son, by Agar, his chamber-maid. And, therefore, there are Saracens that are called Ishmaelites; and some are called Agarenes, of Agar; and others are called Saracens of Sarah; and some are called Moabites, and some Ammonites, from the two sons of Lot, Moab and Ammon, whom he begat on his daughters, and who were afterward great earthly princes.

And also Mohammed loved well a good hermit, who dwelt in the desert a mile from Mount Sinai, in the way from Arabia toward Chaldea and toward India, one day's journey from the sea, where the merchants of Venice come often for merchandise. And so often went Mohammed to this hermit that all his men were angry; for he would gladly hear this hermit preach, and make his men wait all night, and therefore his men thought to put the hermit to death; and so it befell on a night that Mohammed was drunk with good wine, and he fell asleep; and his men took Mohammed's sword out of his sheath, while he slept, and therewith they slew the hermit, and put his sword, all bloody, in his sheath again. And on the morrow, when he found the hermit dead, he was very wroth, and would have put his men to death; but they all with one accord said that he himself had slain him when he was drunk, and showed him his sword all bloody; and he believed that they said truth. And then he cursed the wine and all those that drink it. And therefore Saracens that be devout never drink wine; but some drink it privately; for if they drink it openly they would be reproved. But they drink good beverage, and sweet and nourishing, which is made of galamelle; and that is what men make sugar of, which is of right good savor, and it is good for the breast. Also it happens sometimes that Christians become Saracens, either from poverty or from ignorance, or else from their own wickedness. And therefore the archiflamen, or the flamen, as our archbishop or bishop, when he receives them, says, *La ellec sila, Machomete rores alla;* that is to say, *There is no God but one, and Mohammed His messenger.*

CHAPTER XIII.

OF ALBANIA AND OF LYBIA—OF THE WISHINGS FOR WATCHING OF THE SPARROW-HAWK; AND OF NOAH'S SHIP.

Now, since I have told you before of the Holy Land, and of that country about, and of many ways to go to that land, to Mount Sinai, and of Babylon the Greater and the Less, and other places, now is the time, if it please you, to tell you of the borders and isles, and divers beasts, and of various peoples beyond these borders. For in the countries beyond are many diverse countries, and many great kingdoms, that are separated by the four streams that come from terrestrial Paradise. For Mesopotamia, and the kingdom of Chaldea, and Arabia, are between the two rivers of Tigris and Euphrates. And Media and Persia are between the rivers of Nile and Tigris. And Syria, Palestine, and Phœnicia are between the Euphrates and the Mediterranean Sea, which sea extends in length from Marok, on the Sea of Spain, to the great sea, so that it lasts beyond Constantinople three thousand and forty Lombard miles.

Toward the Ocean Sea, in India, is the kingdom of Scythia, which is inclosed in mountains; and after, below Scythia, from the Caspian Sea to the River Thainy, is Amazonia, or the land of Feminy, where there is no man, but only women. And after is Albania, a full great realm; so called because the people are whiter there than in other countries thereabout. And in that country are so great and strong dogs, that they assail lions and slay them. And then after are Hircania, Bactria, Iberia, and many other kingdoms.

And between the Red Sea and the Ocean Sea, toward the south, is the kingdom of Ethiopia, and Lybia the Higher. Which land of Lybia (that is to say, Lower Lybia) commences at the Sea of Spain, from thence where the Pillars of Hercules are, and extends to Egypt and toward Ethiopia. In that country of Lybia the sea is higher than the land, and it seems that it would cover the earth, and yet it passeth not its bounds. And men see in that country a mountain to which no man cometh. In this land of Lybia, whoso turneth toward the east, the shadow of himself is on the right side, and here, in our country, the shadow is on the left side. In that sea of Lybia is no fish, for they may not live for the great heat of the sun; because the water is ever boiling for the great heat. And many other lands there are that it were too long to tell or to number; but of some parts I shall speak more plainly hereafter.

Whoever will go toward Tartary, Persia, Chaldea, and India, must enter the sea at Genoa, or at Venice, or at some other haven that I have mentioned before, and then pass the sea and arrive at Trebizond, which is a good city; and it was wont to be the haven of Pountz (Pontus). There is the haven of Persians and of Medians, and of the countries beyond.

In that city lieth St. Athanasius, who was bishop of Alexandria, and made the psalm, "Quicunque vult." This Athanasius was a great doctor of divinity; and because he preached and spake so deeply of divinity and of the godhead, he was accused to the Pope of Rome of being a heretic; wherefore the Pope sent after him, and put him in prison, and while he was in prison he made the psalm, and sent it to the Pope, and said, that if he were a heretic that was his heresy; for that, he said, was his belief. And when the Pope saw it, and had examined it that it was perfect and good, and verily our faith and our belief, he set him at liberty, and commanded that psalm to be said every day at prayer; and so he held Athanasius a good man. But he would never go to his bishopric again, because he had been accused of heresy. Trebizond was formerly held by the Emperor of Constantinople; but a great man whom he sent to keep the country against the Turks, usurped the land and held it to himself, and called himself Emperor of Trebizond.

And from thence men go through Little Ermony (Armenia), in which is an old castle, on a rock, called the castle of the Sparrowhawk. It is beyond the city of Layays (Lajazzo), beside the town of Pharsipee, which belongs to the lordship of Cruk, a rich lord and a good Christian. There is found a sparrow-hawk upon a fair perch, and a fair lady of fairie, who keeps it; and whoever will watch that sparrow-hawk seven days and seven nights, and, as some men say, three days and three nights, without company and without sleep, that fair lady shall give him, when he hath done, the first wish that he will wish of earthly things; and that hath been proved oftentimes. And once a king of Ermony, who was a worthy knight and a brave man, and a noble prince, watched that hawk some time; and at the end of seven days and seven nights the lady came to him, and bade him wish, for he had well deserved it; and he answered that he was a great lord enough, and well in peace, and had enough of worldly riches; and therefore he would wish no other thing but the body of that fair lady. And she answered him that he knew not what he asked, and said that he was a fool to desire what he might not have; for she said that he should only ask an earthly thing; and she was no earthly thing, but a spiritual thing. And the king said that he would ask no other thing. And the lady answered, "Since I may not withdraw you from your lewd boldness, I shall give you without wishing, and to all that shall come of you. Sir king, you shall have war without peace, and always, to the ninth degree, you shall be in subjection to your enemies, and you shall be in need of all goods." And since that neither the King of Ermony nor the country was ever in peace or rich; and they have since been always under tribute to the Saracens.

At another time the son of a poor man watched the hawk, and wished that he might have good success, and be fortunate in merchandise. And the lady granted it him, and he became the richest and most famous merchant that might be on sea or on land; and he became so rich that he knew not one-thousandth part of what he had; and he was wiser in wishing than the king. Also a knight of the temple watched there, and wished a purse ever full of gold; and the lady granted him; but she told him that he had asked the destruction of the order; for the trust of that purse, and for the great pride that they should have; and so it was. And therefore let him who watches beware; for if he sleep he is lost, that never man shall see him more. This is not the direct way to go to the parts that I have mentioned before, but to see the marvel of which I have spoken.

And, therefore, whoever will go the direct way must proceed from Trebizond toward Ermony the Great, to a city called Artyroun (Erzeroum) which was formerly a good and populous city, but the Turks have greatly wasted it. Thereabout grows little or no wine or fruit. In this land the earth is higher than in any other; and that makes it very cold. And there are many good waters and good wells, that come under earth from the river of Paradise, which is called Euphrates, which is a day's journey from this city. And that river comes toward India, under earth, and reappears in the land of Altazar. And so men pass by this Ermony, and enter the Sea of Persia.

From that city of Artyroun men go to a mountain called Sabissocolle; and there beside is another mountain called Ararat, but the Jews call it Taneez, where Noah's ship rested, and still is upon that mountain; and men may see it afar in clear weather. That mountain is full seven miles high; and some men say that they have seen and touched the ship, and put their fingers in the parts where the devil went out, when Noah said "Benedicite." But they that say so speak without knowledge; for no one can go up the mountain for the great abundance of snow which is always on that mountain, both summer and winter, so that no man ever went up since the time of Noah, except a monk, who, by God's grace, brought one of the planks down, which is yet in the monastery at the foot of the mountain.

And beside is the city of Dayne, which was founded by Noah, near which is the city of Any, in which were one thousand churches. This monk had great desire to go up that mountain; and so upon a day he went up; and when he had ascended the third part of the mountain he was so weary that he fell asleep; when he awoke he found himself lying at the foot of the mountain. Then he prayed devoutly to God that he would suffer him to go up; and an angel came to him, and said that he should go up; and so he did. And since that time no one ever went up; wherefore men should not believe such words.

From that mountain we go to the city of Thauriso (Tabreez), which was formerly called Taxis, a very fair and great city, and one of the best in the world for merchandise; and it is in the land of the Emperor of Persia. And they say that the emperor receives more in that city for custom of merchandise than the richest Christian king alive from all his realm; for the toll and custom of his merchants is beyond calculation. Beside that city is a hill of salt, of which every man taketh what he will. There dwell many Christians under tribute of Saracens. And from that city men pass by many towns and castles, on the way toward India to the city of Sadony, which is ten days from Thauriso; and it is a very noble and great city. And there the Emperor of Persia dwells in summer, because the climate is temperate. And there are good rivers capable of bearing ships. Then men go the way toward India for many days, and by many countries, to the city called Cassak, a full noble city, abounding in corn, wines, and all other goods.

This is the city where the three kings met together when they went to seek our Lord in Bethlehem, to worship him and to present him with gold, essence, and myrrh. And it is from that city to Bethlehem fifty-three days. From that city men go to another city, called Bethe (Beth-Germa? or Old Bagdad), a day from the sea which they call the Sandy Sea. This is the best city which the Emperor of Persia has in all his land, and it is called there Chardabago; and others call it Vapa. And the pagans say that no Christian may remain long alive in that city; but they die within short time, and no man knows the cause. Afterward men go by many cities and towns and great countries to the city of Cornaa (Kornah?), which was formerly so great that the walls are twenty-five miles about. The walls are still standing, but it is not all inhabited. From Cornaa men go by many lands, and many cities and towns, unto the land of Job; and there ends the land of the Emperor of Persia.

CHAPTER XIV.

OF THE LAND OF JOB, AND OF HIS AGE—OF THE ARRAY OF MEN OF CHALDEA—OF THE LAND WHERE WOMEN DWELL WITHOUT COMPANY OF MEN—OF THE KNOWLEDGE AND VIRTUES OF THE TRUE DIAMOND.

AFTER leaving Cornaa we enter the land of Job, a very fair country, and abounding in all goods; and men call it the land of Sweze (Susiana). In that land is the city of Theman. Job was a pagan, and he was son of Are of Gosre, and held the land as prince of the country; and he was so rich that he knew not the hundredth part of his goods. And, although he was a pagan, still he served God well, after his law; and our Lord took his service in satisfaction. And when he fell in poverty he was seventy-eight years of age. And afterward, when God had tried his patience, which was so great, he brought him again to riches and to higher estate than before. And after that he was King of Idumea, after King Esau. And when he was king he was called Jobab. And in that kingdom he lived afterward one hundred and seventy years; and so he was of age, when he died, two hundred and forty-eight years.

In that land of Job there is no want of anything needful to man's body. There are hills, where they get manna in greater abundance than in any other country. This manna is called bread of angels; and it is a white thing, very sweet and delicious, and sweeter than honey or sugar; it comes of the dew of heaven, that falls upon the herbs in that country; and it congeals, and becomes white and sweet; and they put it in medicine for rich men, for it cleanseth the blood and putteth out melancholy.

This land of Job borders on the kingdom of Chaldea. This land of Chaldea is very extensive; and the language of that country is greater in sounding than it is in other parts beyond the sea. We pass it to go to the tower of Babylon the Great, of which I have spoken, where all the languages were first changed; and that is four days from Chaldea. In that realm are fair men, and they go full nobly arrayed in cloths of gold, or frayed, and appareled with great pearls and precious stones full nobly; but the women are very ugly and vilely arrayed; and they go barefoot, and clothed in evil garments, large and wide, but short to the knees, and long sleeves down to the feet, like a monk's frock, and their sleeves are hanging about their shoulders; and they are black women, foul and hideous; and truly they are as bad as they are foul.

In that kingdom of Chaldea, in a city called Ur, dwelt Terah, Abraham's father; and there was Abraham born, which was in the time that Ninus was King of Babylon, of Arabia and of Egypt. This Ninus made the city of Nineveh, which Noah had begun; and because Ninus completed it, he called it Nineveh after his own name. There lies Tobit the prophet, of whom Holy Writ speaketh. And from that city of Ur Abraham departed, by the commandment of God, after the death of his father, and led him Sarah, his wife, and Lot, his brother's son, because he had no child. And they went to dwell in the land of Canaan, in a place called Sechem. And this Lot was he who was saved, when Sodom and Gomorrah and the other cities, where the Dead Sea now is, were burned and sunk down to hell, as I have told you before.

Beside the land of Chaldea is the land of Amazonia, in which is all women, and no man; not, as some men say, because men may not live there, but because the women will not suffer men amongst them, to be their sovereigns. This land of Amazon is an island surrounded by the sea, except in two places, where are two entrances. And beyond the water dwell the men who are their paramours, where they go to solace them when they will. Beside Amazonia is the land of Tarmegyte, a great and very pleasant country, and for the goodness of which king Alexander made there the city of Alexandria; he made twelve cities of the same name, but that city is now called Celsite. And from that other side of Chaldea, toward the south, is Ethiopia, a great country which extends to the extremity of Egypt.

Ethiopia is divided into two principal parts, the east and the south, the latter part being called Mauritania. And the people of that country are blacker than in the other part, and are called Moors. In that country is a well, which in the day is so cold that no man may drink thereof, and in the night it is so hot that no man may suffer his hand therein. Toward the south, to pass by the Ocean Sea, is a great country, but men may not dwell there, for the fervent burning of the sun. In Ethiopia all the rivers and waters are troubled, and somewhat salt, for the great heat that is there.

And the people of that country are easily intoxicated, and have but little appetite for meat. And they are afflicted with dysenteries, and live not long. In Ethiopia, the children, when young, are all yellow; and when they grow older that yellowness turns to black. In Ethiopia is the city of Saba and the land where one of the three kings reigned who came to our Lord in Bethlehem.

From Ethiopia they go to India through many different countries; and men call the higher India Emlak. India is divided into three principal parts, the Greater, which is a very hot country; and India the Less, which is a temperate country, extending to the land of Media, and the third part, toward the north, is so cold, that for continual frost the water becomes crystal; and upon those rocks of crystal grow the good diamonds, that are of troubled color. Yellow crystal draws color like oil. And they are so hard that no man may polish them; and men call them diamonds in that country, and *hamese* in another country.

Other diamonds are found in Arabia, but they are not so good; they are browner and more tender. And other diamonds also are found in the Island of Cyprus, which are still more tender, and may easily be polished; and they find diamonds also in Macedonia; but the best and most precious are in India. And they often find hard diamonds in a mass which comes out of gold, when they break the mass in small pieces, to purify it and refine it, out of the mine. And it sometimes happens that they find some as great as a pea, and some less; and they are as hard as those of India. And although men find good diamonds in India, yet nevertheless men find them more commonly upon the rocks in the sea, and upon hills where the mine of gold is. They grow many together, one little, another great; and there are some of the greatness of a bean, and some as great as a hazel nut. They are square and pointed of their own kind, both above and beneath, without work of man's hand; and they grow together, male and female, and are nourished by the dew of heaven; and they engender commonly and bring forth small children, that multiply and grow all the year. I have oftentimes tried the experiment, that if a man keep them with a little of the rock, and wet them with May-dew often, they shall grow every year, and the small will grow great; for right as the fine pearl congeals and grows great by the dew of heaven, right so doth the true diamond; and right as the pearl of its own nature takes roundness, so the diamond, by virtue of God, takes squareness.

And a man should carry the diamond on his left side, for it is of greater virtue than on the right side; for the strength of their growing is toward the north, that is the left side of the world; and the left part of man is when he turns his face toward the east. And if you wish to know the virtues of the diamond (as men may find in the "Lapidary," with which many men are not acquainted), I shall tell you, as they beyond the sea say and affirm, from whom, all science and philosophy comes. He who carries the diamond upon him, it gives him hardiness and manhood, and it keeps the limbs of his body whole. It gives him victory over his enemies in court and in war, if his cause be just; and it keeps him that bears it in good wit; and it keeps him from strife and riot, from sorrows and from enchantments, and from fantasies and illusions of wicked spirits. And if any cursed witch or enchanter would bewitch him that bears the diamond, all that sorrow and mischance shall turn to the offender, through virtue of that stone; and also no wild beast dare assail the man who bears it on him. Also the diamond should be given freely, without coveting and without buying, and then it is of greater virtue; and it makes a man stronger and firmer against his enemies; and heals him that is lunatic, and those whom the fiend pursues or torments. And if venom or poison be brought in presence of the diamond, anon it begins to grow moist and sweat.

There are also diamonds in India that are called violastres (for their color is like violet, or more brown than violets), that are very hard and precious, but some men like them not so well as the others. Also there is another kind of diamonds that are as white as crystal; but they are a little more troubled; and they are good and of great virtue, and they are all square and pointed of their own nature; and some are six-square, some four-square, and some three, as nature shapes them; and, therefore, when great lords and knights go to seek honor in arms, they gladly bear the diamond upon them.

I shall speak a little more of the diamonds, that they who know them not may not be deceived by chapmen who go through the country selling them; for whoever will buy the diamond, it is needful that he know them, because men counterfeit them often with crystal, which is yellow; and with sapphires of citron-color, which is yellow also; and with the sapphire loupe, and with many other stones. But these counterfeits are not so hard; and the points will break easily, and men may easily polish them. But some workmen, for malice, will not polish them, to that intent, to make men believe that they may not be polished. But men may assay them in this manner: first cut with them or write with them in sapphires, in crystal, or in other precious stones. Also take the adamant, that is, the shipman's stone, that draws the needle to it, and lay the diamond on it, and lay the needle before the adamant; and if the diamond be good and virtuous, the adamant draws not the needle, while the diamond is there present. This is the proof that they beyond the sea use. Nevertheless it happens often that the good diamond loses its virtue by sin, and for incontinence of him that bears it; and then it is needful to make it recover its virtue again, or else it is of little value.

CHAPTER XV.

OF THE CUSTOMS OF ISLES ABOUT INDIA—OF THE DIFFERENCE BETWEEN IDOLS AND SIMULACRES—OF THREE KINDS OF PEPPER GROWING UPON ONE TREE—OF THE WELL THAT CHANGES ITS ODOR EVERY HOUR OF THE DAY.

In India are very many different countries; and it is called India, from a river which runs through the country called Indus. In that river they find eels thirty feet long and more. And the people that dwell near that river are of evil color, green and yellow. In India, and about India, are more than five thousand inhabited islands, good and great, besides those that are uninhabitable, and other small islands. Every island has great plenty of cities, and towns, and people without number. For men of India have this condition of nature, that they never go out of their own country, and therefore there is great multitude of people; but they are not stirring or movable, because they are in the first climate, that is, of Saturn.

And Saturn is slow, and little moving; for he tarrieth thirty years to make his course through the twelve signs; and the moon passes through the twelve signs in a month. And because Saturn is so slow of motion, the people of that country, that are under his climate, have no inclination or will to move or stir to seek strange places. Our country is all the contrary; for we are in the seventh climate, which is of the moon, and the moon moves rapidly, and is a planet of progression; and for that reason it gives us a natural will to move lightly, and to go different ways, and to seek strange things and other diversities of the world; for the moon goes round the earth more rapidly than any other planet.

Also men go through India by many different countries, to the great Sea of Ocean. And afterward men find there an island that is called Hermes; and there come merchants of Venice and Genoa, and of other parts, to buy merchandise; but there is great heat in that district. In that country, and in Ethiopia, and in many other countries, the inhabitants lie all naked in rivers and waters, men and women together, from undurn of the day till it be past noon. And they lie all in the water, except the face, for the great heat that there is. And the women have no shame of the men, but lie all together, side by side, till the heat is past. There may men see many foul figures assembled, and chiefly near the good towns. In that island are ships without nails of iron or bonds, on account of the rocks of adamants (loadstones); for they are all abundant thereabout in that sea, that it is marvelous to speak of; and if a ship passed there that had either iron bonds or iron nails, it would perish; for the adamant, by its nature, draws iron to it; and so it would draw to it the ship, because of the iron, that it should never depart from it.

From that island men go by sea to another island called Chana, where is abundance of corn and wine; and it was wont to be a great island, and a great and good haven, but the sea has greatly wasted and overcome it. The king of that country was formerly so strong and so mighty that he held war against King Alexander. The people of that country differ in their religious belief; for some worship the sun, some the moon, some the fire, some trees, some serpents, or the first thing that they meet in a morning; and some worship simulacres, and some idols.

Between simulacres and idols there is a great difference; for simulacres are images made after the likeness of men or of women, or of the sun or of the moon, or of any beast, or of any natural thing; and an idol is an image made by the lewd will of man, which is not to be found among natural things, as an image that has four heads, one of a man, another of a horse, or of an ox, or of some other beasts, that no man has seen in nature. And they that worship simulacres worship them for some worthy man who once existed, as Hercules and many others, that did many wonders in their time.

For they say well that they are not gods; for they know well that there is a God of nature that made all things, who is in heaven; but they know well that this man may not do the wonders that he did, unless it had been by the special gift of God, and therefore they say that he was well with God, wherefore they worship him. And so they say of the sun; because it changes the season and gives heat and nourishes all things upon earth; and since it is of so great profit, they know well that they might not be, unless God loved it more than any other thing. And because God has given it greater virtue in the world, therefore it is right, as they say, to worship and reverence it. And so they say of other planets, and of the fire also, because it is so profitable.

And of idols, they say also that the ox is the most holy beast that is on earth, and more patient and more profitable than any other; and they know well that it may not be without special grace of God, and therefore make they their god of an ox the one part, and the other part of a man, because man is the noblest creature on earth, and also he hath lordship above all beasts; therefore make they the upper half of the idol of a man, and the lower half of an ox; and so of serpents and of other beasts, and different things that they worship, that they meet first in a morning. And they worship also especially all those that they have good meeting of, and when they speed well in their journey, after their meeting, and mostly such as they have proved and assayed by experience of long time; for they say that that good meeting may not come but by the grace of God; and therefore they make images like to those things in which they have belief, to behold them and worship them first in the morning, before they meet any contrarious thing.

And there are also some Christians who say that it is good to meet some beasts first in the morning, and bad to meet others; and that they have often proved that it is very unlucky to meet the hare, the swine, and many other beasts; and the sparrow-hawk, and other ravenous birds, when they fly after their prey, and take it before armed men, is a good sign, and if they fail of taking their prey it is an evil sign; and also, to such people it is unlucky to meet ravens. There are many people that believe in these things, and in other such, because it happens often so to fall after their fantasies; and also there are men enough that disbelieve in them. And since Christians have such belief, who are instructed and taught all day by holy doctrine wherein they should believe, it is no wonder that the pagans, who have no good doctrine but only of their nature, believe more largely, on account of their simplicity.

And truly I have seen pagans and Saracens, whom men call augurs, that when we ride in arms in different countries against our enemies, they would tell us, by the flight of birds, the prognostications of things that fell after; and so they did full often, and offered to pledge their heads that it would fall as they said. But a man should not, therefore, put his belief in such things, but always have full trust and belief in God our sovereign lord. The Saracens have won and now hold this Island of Chana. It contains many lions, and many other wild beasts, with rats as great as dogs, which they take with great mastiffs, for cats can not take them. In this island, and many others, they do not bury their dead; for the heat is so great, that in a little time the flesh will consume from the bones.

From thence men go by sea toward India the Greater, to a good and fair city called Sarche, where dwell many Christians of good faith; and there are many monks, especially mendicants. Thence men go by sea to the land of Lomb, in which grows the pepper, in the forest called Combar, and it grows nowhere else in all the world; that forest extends full eighteen days in length. In the forest are two good cities, one called Fladrine, and the other Zinglantz, in each of which dwell many Christians and Jews; for it is a good and rich country, but the heat is exceeding.

And you shall understand that the pepper grows like a wild vine, which is planted close by the trees of that wood, to sustain it; the fruit hangs like bunches of grapes, with which the tree is so laden that it seems that it would break; and when it is ripe, it is all green like ivy berries; and then men cut them as they do the vines, and put them upon an oven, where they become black and crisp. There are three kinds of pepper all on one tree; long pepper, black pepper, and white pepper. The long pepper is called Sorbotin; the black is called Fulful; and the white is called Bano. The long pepper comes first, when the leaf begins to appear, and is like the catkins of hazel that come before the leaf, and it hangs low. Next comes the black with the leaf, like clusters of grapes, all green; and, when gathered, it becomes the white, which is somewhat less than the black, and of that but little is brought to this country, for they keep it for themselves, because it is better and milder than the black.

In that country are many kinds of serpents and other vermin, in consequence of the great heat of the country and of the pepper. And some men say that, when they will gather the pepper, they make fires and burn thereabouts, to make the serpents and cockodrills to fly; but this is not true. But thus they do: they anoint their hands and feet with a juice made of snails and other things, of which the serpents and venomous beasts hate the savor; and that makes them fly before them, because of the smell, and then they gather in the pepper in safety.

Toward the head of that forest is the city of Polombe, above which is a great mountain, also called Polombe, from which the city has its name. And at the foot of that mountain is a fair and great well, which has the odor and savor of all spices; and at every hour of the day it changes its odor and savor diversely; and whoever drinks three times fasting of the water of that well is whole of all kind of sickness that he has; and they that dwell there, and drink often of that well, never have sickness, but appear always young. I have drunk thereof three or four times, and methinks I still fare the better. Some men call it the Well of Youth; for they that often drink thereof appear always young, and live without sickness. And men say that that well comes out of Paradise, and therefore it is so virtuous.

All that country grows good ginger; and therefore merchants go thither for spicery. In that land men worship the ox, for his simpleness and for his meekness, and for the profit that comes of him. They say that he is the holiest beast on earth; for they consider that whosoever is meek and patient, he is holy and profitable, for then, they say, he hath all virtues in him. They make the ox to labor six or seven years, and then they eat him.

In that country they make idols, half man, half ox; and in those idols evil spirits speak, and even answer to men. Before these idols men often slay their children, and sprinkle the blood on the idols, and so they make their sacrifice. And when any man dies in the country they burn his body in the name of penance, to that intent that he suffer no pain in earth, by being eaten by worms. And if his wife have no child they burn her with him, and say that it is right that she accompany him in the other world as she did in this. But if she have children with him, they let her live with them, to bring them up, if she will. And if she love more to live with her children than to die with her husband, they hold her for false and cursed; and she shall never be loved or trusted by the people. And if the woman die before the husband, they burn him with her, if he will; and if he will not, no man constraineth him thereto, but he may wed another time without blame or reproof. In that country grow many strong vines, and the women drink wine, and men not; and the women shave their beards, and the men not.

CHAPTER XVI.

OF THE JUDGMENTS MADE BY ST. THOMAS—OF DEVOTION AND SACRIFICE MADE TO IDOLS THERE, IN THE CITY OF CALAMY; AND THE PROCESSION ABOUT THE CITY.

FROM that country we pass many districts toward a country ten days' journey thence, called Mabaron, which is a great kingdom, containing many fair cities and towns. In that kingdom lies the body of St. Thomas the Apostle, in flesh and bone, in a fair tomb, in the city of Calamy; for there he was martyred and buried. But men of Assyria carried his body into Mesopotamia, into the city of Edessa; and, afterward, he was brought thither again. And the arm and the hand that he put in our Lord's side, when He appeared to him after His resurrection, is yet lying in a vessel without the tomb. By that hand they there make all their judgments. For when there is any dissention between two parties, and each of them maintain his cause, both parties write their causes in two bills, and put them in the hand of St. Thomas; and anon he casts away the bill of the wrong cause, and holds still the bill with the right cause. And, therefore, men come from far countries to have judgment of doubtful causes.

The church where St. Thomas lies is both great and fair, and full of great simulacres, which are great images that they call their gods, of which the least is as great as two men. And, amongst the others, there is a great image larger than any of the others, all covered with fine gold and precious stones and rich pearls; and that idol is the god of false Christians, who have renounced their faith. It sits in a chair of gold, very nobly arrayed, and has about the neck large girdles made of gold and precious stones and pearls. The church is full richly wrought, and gilt all over within. And to that idol men go on pilgrimage, as commonly and with as great devotion as Christian men go to St. James, or other holy pilgrimages. And many people that come from far lands to seek that idol, for the great devotion that they have, never look upward, but evermore down to the earth, for dread to see anything about them that should hinder them of their devotion. And some who go on pilgrimage to this idol bear knives in their hands, that are very keen and sharp, and continually, as they go, they smite themselves on their arms, legs, and thighs, with many hideous wounds; and so they shed their blood for love of that idol. They say that he is blessed and holy that dieth so for love of his god. And others there are who carry their children to be slain as a sacrifice to that idol; and after they have slain them, they sprinkle the blood upon the idol. And some, who come from far, in going toward this idol, at every third pass that they go from their home, they kneel, and so continue till they come thither; and when they come there, they take incense and other aromatic things of noble smell, and scent the idol, as we here do God's precious body.

And so people come to worship this image, some a hundred miles, and some many more. And before the minster of this idol is a pool, like a great lake, full of water; and therein pilgrims cast gold and silver, pearls and precious stones, without number, instead of offerings. And when the ministers of that church need to make any reparation of the church or of any of the idols, they take gold and silver, pearls and precious stones, out of the pond, to pay the expenses of such thing as they make or repair. At great feasts and solemnities of that idol, as the dedication of the church and the enthroning of the idol, all the country about meet there, and set the idol upon a chair with great reverence, well arrayed with cloths of gold, of rich cloths of Tartary, of camaka, and other precious cloths; and they lead him about the city with great solemnity. And before the chair go first in procession all the maidens of the country, two and two together; and, after them, the pilgrims. And some of them fall down under the wheels of the chair, and let the chair go over them, so that they die immediately. And some have their arms or their limbs broken. And all this they do. for love of their god, in great devotion. And they think that the more pain and tribulation they suffer for love of their god, the more joy they shall have in another world. In a word, they suffer so great pains and so hard martyrdoms for love of their idol, that a Christian, I believe, durst not take upon him the tenth part of the pain for love of our Lord Jesus Christ. And after them before the chair, go all the minstrels of the country, with divers instruments, and make all the melody they can.

And when they have all gone about the city they return to the minster and put the idol again into its place. And then, for the love and in worship of that idol, and for the reverence of the feast, two hundred or three hundred persons slay themselves with sharp knives, whose bodies they bring before the idol; and then they say that those are saints, because they slew themselves of their own good will, for love of their idol. And as men here, that had a holy saint of their kin, would think that it was to them a high worship, right so they think there. And as men here devoutly would write holy saints' lives and their miracles, and sue for their canonizations, right so do they there for them that slay themselves voluntarily for love of their idol. And they say that they are glorious martyrs and saints, and put them in their writings and in their litanies, and boast them greatly one to another of their holy kinsmen, that so became saints, and say, " I have more holy saints in my family than thou in thine."

And the custom also there is this, that when any one has such devotion and intent to slay himself for love of his god, they send for all their friends, and have numerous minstrels, and they go before the idol, leading him that will slay himself for such devotion, between them, with great reverence. And he, all naked, hath a very sharp knife in his hand, and he cuts a great piece of his flesh and casts it in the face of his idol, saying his prayers, recommending himself to his god; and then he smites himself, and makes great wounds and deep here and there, till he falls down dead. And then his friends present his body to the idol; and then they say, singing, "Holy god, behold what thy true servant hath done for thee; he hath forsaken his wife, and his children, and his riches, and all the goods of the world and his own life for the love of thee, and to make for thee sacrifice of his flesh and of his blood. Wherefore, holy god, put him amongst thy best beloved saints in thy bliss of paradise, for he hath well deserved it." Then they make a great fire, and burn the body; and then every one of his friends takes a quantity of the ashes, and keeps them instead of relics, saying that it is a holy thing; and they dread no peril while they have the holy ashes upon them. And they put his name in their litanies as a saint.

CHAPTER XVII.

OF THE EVIL CUSTOMS IN THE ISLE OF LAMARY; AND HOW THE EARTH AND THE SEA ARE OF ROUND FORM, AS IS PROVED BY THE STAR CALLED ANTARCTIC, WHICH IS FIXED IN THE SOUTH.

From that country men go by the Sea of Ocean, and by many divers isles and countries which it would be too long to describe. Fifty-two days from the land I have spoken of there is another extensive land, which they call Lamary, in which the heat is very great; and it is the custom there for men and women to go all naked. And they scorn when they see foreigners going clothed, because they say that God made Adam and Eve all naked, and that no man should be ashamed of what is according to nature. And they say that they that are clothed are people of another world, or people who believe not in God. And they marry there no wives, for all the women are common; and they say they sin if they refuse any man: for God commanded Adam and Eve, and all that come of him, that they should increase and multiply and fill the land, therefore may no man in that country say, "This is my wife;" and no woman may say, "This is my husband." And when they have children they may give them to what man they will, who has companied with them. And all land and property also is common, nothing being shut up, or kept under lock, one man being as rich as another. But in that country there is a cursed custom, for they eat more gladly man's flesh than any other flesh, although their country abounds in flesh, fish, corn, gold, and silver, and all other goods. Thither merchants go, who bring with them children to sell to them of the country, and they buy them; and if they are fat they eat them anon; and if they are lean they feed them till they are fat, and then eat them; and they say that it is the best and sweetest flesh in the world.

Neither in that land, nor in many others beyond it, may any man see the polar star, which is called the Star of the Sea, which is immovable, and is toward the north, and which we call the load-star. But they see another star opposite to it, toward the south, which is called antarctic. And right as shipmen here govern themselves by the load-star, so shipmen beyond these parts are guided by the star of the south, which appears not to us. This star, which is toward the north, what we call the load-star, appears not to them. For which cause, we may clearly perceive that the land and sea are of round shape and form, because the part of the firmament appears in one country which is not seen in another country.

And men may prove by experience and their understanding, that if a man found passages by ships, he might go by ship all round the world above and beneath; which I prove thus, after what I have seen. For I have been toward the parts of Brabant, and found by the astrolabe that the polar star is fifty-three degrees high; and further, in Germany and Bohemia, it has fifty-eight degrees; and still further toward the north it is sixty-two degrees and some minutes; for I myself have measured it by the astrolabe. Now you shall know that opposite the polar star is the other star, called antarctic, as I have said before. These two stars are fixed; and about them all the firmament turns as a wheel that turns on its axle-tree; so that those stars bear the firmament in two equal parts; so that it has as much above as it has beneath. After this I have gone toward the south, and have found that in Lybia we first see the antarctic star; and I have gone so far in those countries that I have found that star higher, so that, toward Upper Lybia, it is eighteen degrees and certain minutes. After going by sea and land toward the country of which I spoke last, and to other isles and lands beyond that country, I have found the antarctic star thirty-three degrees in latitude, and some minutes. And if I had had company and shipping to go further, I believe certainly that we should have seen all the roundness of the firmament all about.

For, as I have told you before, the half of the firmament is between the two stars, which half I have seen. And the other half I have seen toward the north, under the polar star, sixty-two degrees and ten minutes; and, toward the south, I have seen under the antarctic thirty-three degrees and sixteen minutes; and the half of the firmament in all contains but one hundred and eighty degrees, of which I have seen sixty-two on the one part, and thirty-three on the other, which makes ninety-five degrees and nearly the half of a degree; so that I have seen all the firmament except eighty-four degrees and the half of a degree; and that is not the fourth part of the firmament. By which I tell you, certainly, that men may go all round the world, as well under as above, and return to their country, if they had company, and shipping, and guides; and always they would find men, lands, and isles, as well as in our part of the world. For they who are toward the antarctic are directly feet opposite feet of them who dwell under the polar star; as well as we and they that dwell under us are feet opposite feet. For all parts of sea and land have their opposites, habitable or passable.

And know well that, after what I may perceive and understand, the lands of Prester John, Emperor of India, are under us; for in going from Scotland or from England, toward Jerusalem, men go always upward; for our land is in the low part of the earth, toward the west; and the land of Prester John is in the low part of the earth, toward the east; and they have there the day when we have night; and, on the contrary, they have the night when we have the day; for the earth and the sea are of a round form, as I have said before; and as men go upward to one part, they go downward to another. Also you have heard me say that Jerusalem is in the middle of the world; and that may be proved and shown there by a spear which is fixed in the earth at the hour of midday, when it is equinoctial, which gives no shadow on any side.

They, therefore, that start from the west to go toward Jerusalem, as many days as they go upward to go thither, in so many days may they go from Jerusalem to other confines of the superficialities of the earth beyond. And when men go beyond that distance, toward India and to the foreign isles, they are proceeding on the roundness of the earth and the sea, under our country. And therefore hath it befallen many times of a thing that I have heard told when I was young, how a worthy man departed once from our country to go and discover the world; and so he passed India, and the isles beyond India, where are more than five thousand isles; and so long he went by sea and land, and so environed the world by many seasons, that he found an isle where he heard people speak his own language, calling an oxen in the plow such words as men speak to beasts in his own country, whereof he had great wonder, for he knew not how it might be. But I say that he had gone so long, by land and sea, that he had gone all round the earth, that he was come again to his own borders, if he would have passed forth till he had found his native country. But he turned again from thence, from whence he was come; and so he lost much painful labor, as himself said, a great while after, when he was coming home; for it befell after, that he went into Norway, and the tempest of the sea carried him to an isle; and when he was in that isle he knew well that it was the isle where he had heard his own language spoken before, and the calling of the oxen at the plow.

But it seems to simple and unlearned men that men may not go under the earth, but that they would fall from under toward the heaven. But that may not be any more than we fall toward heaven from the earth where we are; for from what part of the earth that men dwell, either above or beneath, it seems always to them that they go more right than any other people. And right as it seems to us that they be under us, so it seems to them that we are under them; for if a man might fall from the earth unto the firmament, by greater reason the earth and the sea, that are so great and so heavy, should fall to the firmament; but that may not be, and therefore saith our Lord God, "He haugeth the earth upon nothing."

And although it be possible so to go all round the world, yet of a thousand persons not one might happen to return to his country; for, from the greatness of the earth and sea, men may go by a thousand different ways, that no one could be sure of returning exactly to the parts he came from, unless by chance or by the grace of God; for the earth is very large, and contains in roundness and circuit, above and beneath, 20,425 miles, after the opinion of the old wise astronomers; and, after my little wit, it seems to me, saving their reverence, that it is more; for I say thus: let there be imagined a figure that has a great compass, and, about the point of the great compass, which is called the center, let there be made another little compass; then, afterward, let the great compass be divided by lines in many parts, and all the lines meet at the center; so that in as many parts as the great compass shall be divided, in so many shall the little one that is about the center be divided, although the spaces be less. Let the great compass be represented for the firmament, and the little compass for the earth; now the firmament is divided by astronomers into twelve signs, and every sign is divided into thirty degrees. Also let the earth be divided into as many parts as the firmament, and let every part answer to a degree of the firmament; and I know well that, after the authorities in astronomy, seven hundred furlongs of earth answer to a degree of the firmament, that is eighty-seven miles and four furlongs. Now, multiplied by three hundred and sixty times, it makes 31,500 miles, each of eight furlongs, according to miles of our country. So much hath the earth in circuit after my opinion and understanding.

CHAPTER XVIII.

OF THE PALACE OF THE KING OF THE ISLE OF JAVA—OF THE TREES THAT BEAR MEAL, HONEY, WINE, AND VENOM; AND OF OTHER WONDERS AND CUSTOMS IN THE ISLES THEREABOUTS.

BESIDE the isle I have spoken of, there is another great isle called Sumobor, the king of which is very mighty. The people of that isle make marks in their faces with a hot iron, both men and women, as a mark of great nobility, to be known from other people; for they hold themselves most noble and most worthy of all the world. They have war always with the people that go all naked. Fast beside is another rich isle called Beteinga. And there are many other isles thereabout.

Fast beside that isle, to pass by sea, is a great isle and extensive country called Java, which is near two thousand miles in circuit. And the king of that country is a very great lord, rich and mighty, having under him seven other kings of seven other surrounding isles. This isle is well inhabited, and in it grow all kinds of spices more plentifully than in any other country, as ginger, cloves, canel, sedewalle, nutmegs, and maces. And know well that the nutmeg bears the maces; for right as the nut of the hazel hath a husk in which the nut is inclosed till it be ripe, so it is of the nutmeg and of the maces. Many other spices and many other goods grow in that isle; for of all things there is plenty, except wine. Gold and silver are very plentiful.

The king of that country has a very noble and wonderful palace, and richer than any in the world; for all the steps leading to halls and chambers are alternately of gold and silver; and the pavements of halls and chambers are squares of gold and silver; and all the walls within are covered with gold and silver in thin plates; in which plates are inlaid stories and battles of knights, the crowns and circles about whose heads are made of precious stones and rich and great pearls. And the halls and the chambers of the palace are all covered within with gold and silver, so that no man would believe the richness of that palace unless he had seen it. And know well that the king of that isle is so mighty, that he hath many times overcome the Great Chan of Cathay in battle, who is the greatest emperor under the firmament, either beyond the sea or on this side; for they have often had war between them, because the Great Chan would oblige him to hold his land of him; but the other at all times defendeth himself well against him.

After that isle is another large isle, called Pathan, which is a great kingdom, full of fair cities and towns. In that land grow trees that bear meal, of which men make good bread, white, and of good savor; and it seemeth as it were of wheat, but it is not quite of such savor. And there are other trees that bear good and sweet honey; and others that bear poison, against which there is no medicine but one; and that is to take their own leaves, and stamp them and mix them with water, and then drink it, for no medicine will avail. The Jews had sent for some of this poison by one of their friends, to poison all Christendom, as I have heard them say in their confession before dying; but, thanked be Almighty God, they failed of their purpose, although they caused a great mortality of people. And there are other trees that bear excellent wine.

And if you like to hear how the meal comes out of the trees, men hew the trees with a hatchet, all about the foot, till the bark be separated in many parts; and then comes out a thick liquor, which they receive in vessels, and dry it in the sun; and then carry it to a mill to grind, and it becomes fair and white meal; and the honey, and the wine, and the poison, are drawn out of other trees in the same manner, and put in vessels to keep. In that isle is a dead sea, or lake, that has no bottom; and if anything fall into it, it will never come up again. In that lake grow reeds, which they call Thaby, that are thirty fathoms long; and of these reeds they make fair houses. And there are other reeds, not so long, that grow near the land, and have roots full a quarter of a furlong or more long, at the knots of which roots precious stones are found that have great virtues; for he who carries any of them upon him may not be hurt by iron or steel; and therefore they who have those stones on them fight very boldly both on sea and land; and, therefore, when their enemies are aware of this, they shoot at them arrows and darts without iron or steel, and so hurt and slay them. And also of those reeds they make houses and ships, and other things, as we here make houses and ships of oak, or of any other trees. And let no man think that I am joking, for I have seen these reeds with my own eyes many times, lying upon the river of that lake, of which twenty of our fellows might not lift up or bear one to the earth.

Beyond this isle men go by sea to another rich isle, called Calonak, the king of which has as many wives as he will; for he makes search through the country for the fairest maidens that may be found, who are brought before him, and he taketh one one night, and another another, and so forth in succession; so that he hath a thousand wives or more. Thus the king has many children, sometimes a hundred, sometimes two hundred, and sometimes more. He hath also as many as fourteen thousand elephants, or more, which are brought up amongst his serfs in all his towns. And in case he has war with any of the kings around him, he causes certain men of arms to go up into wooden castles, which are set upon the elephants' backs, to fight against their enemies; and so do other kings thereabouts; and they call the elephants *warkes*.

And in that isle there is a great wonder; for all kinds of fish that are there in the sea come once a year, one kind after the other, to the coast of that isle in so great a multitude that a man can see hardly anything but fish; and there they remain three days; and every man of the country takes as many of them as he likes. And that kind of fish, after the third day, departs and goes into the sea. And after them come another multitude of fish of another kind, and do in the same manner as the first did another three days; and so on with the other kinds, till all the divers kinds of fishes have been there, and men have taken what they like of them. And no man knows the cause; but they of the country say that it is to do reverence to their king, who is the most worthy king in the world, as they say, because he fulfills the commandment of God to Adam and Eve, "Increase and multiply, and fill the earth;" and because he multiplies so the world with children, therefore God sends him the fishes of divers kinds, to take at his will for him and all his people; and thus all the fishes of the sea come to do him homage as the most noble and excellent king of the world, and that is best beloved of God, as they say.

They are also in that country a kind of snails, so great that many persons may lodge in their shells, as men would do in a little house. And there are other snails that are very great, but not so huge as the other, of which, and of great white serpents with black heads, that are as great as a man's thigh, and some less, they make royal meats for the king and other great lords. And if a man who is married die in that country they bury his wife alive with him, for they say that it is right that she make him company in the other world, as she did in this.

From that country they go by the Sea of Ocean, by an isle called Caffolos; the natives of which, when their friends are sick, hang them on trees, and say that it is better that birds, which are angels of God, eat them, than the foul worms of the earth. Then we come to another isle, the inhabitants of which are of full cursed kind, for they breed great dogs, and teach them to strangle their friends, when they are sick, for they will not let them die of natural death; for they say that they should suffer great pain if they abide to die by themselves, as nature would; and, when they are thus strangled, they eat their flesh as though it were venison.

Afterward men go by many isles by sea to an isle called Milk, where are very cursed people; for they delight in nothing more than to fight and slay men; and they drink most gladly man's blood, which they call Dieu. And the more men that a man may slay, the more worship he hath amongst them. And thence they go by sea, from isle to isle, to an isle called Tracoda, the inhabitants of which are as beasts, and unreasonable, and dwell in caves which they make in the earth, for they have not sense to make houses. And when they see any man passing through their countries they hide them in their caves. And they eat flesh of serpents, and speak naught, but hiss, as serpents do.

After that isle, men go by the Sea of Ocean, by many isles, to a great and fair isle called Nacumera, which is in circuit more than a thousand miles. And all the men and women of that isle have dogs' heads; and they are reasonable and of good understanding, except that they worship an ox for their god. And also every man of them beareth an ox of gold or silver on his forehead, in token that they love well their god. And they go all naked, except a little clout, and are large men and warlike, having a great target that covers all the body, and a spear in their hand to fight with. And if they take any man in battle they eat him. The king is rich and powerful, and very devout after his law; and he has about his neck three hundred orient pearls, knotted, as paternosters are here of amber. And as we say our *Pater Noster* and *Ave Maria*, counting the paternosters right, so this king says every day devoutly three hundred prayers to his god, before he eats; and he beareth also about his neck an orient ruby, noble and fine, which is a foot in length, and five fingers large.

And when they choose their king, they give him that ruby to carry in his hand, and so they lead him riding all about the city. And that ruby he shall bear always about his neck; for if he had not that ruby upon him they would not hold him for king. The Chan of Cathay has greatly coveted that ruby, but he might never have it, neither for war, nor for any manner of goods. This king is so righteous and equitable in his judgments, that men may go safely through all his country, and bear with them what they like, and no man shall be bold enough to rob them.

Hence men go to another isle called Silha, which is full eight hundred miles in circuit. In that land is much waste, for it is so full of serpents, dragons, and cockodrills, that no man dare dwell there. These cockodrills are serpents, yellow and rayed above, having four feet, and short thighs, and great nails like claws; and some are five fathoms in length, and some of six, eight, or even ten; and when they go by places that are gravelly, it appears as if men had drawn a great tree through the gravelly place. And there are also many wild beasts, especially elephants.

In that isle is a great mountain, in the midst of which is a large lake in a full fair plain, and there is great plenty of water. And they of the country say that Adam and Eve wept on that mount a hundred years, when they were driven out of Paradise. And that water, they say, is of their tears; for so much water they wept, that made the aforesaid lake. And at the bottom of that lake are found many precious stones and great pearls. In that lake grow many reeds and great canes, and there within are many cockodrills and serpents, and great water-leeches. And the king of that country, once every year, gives leave to poor men to go into the lake to gather precious stones and pearls, by way of alms, for the love of God, that made Adam. To guard against the vermin, they anoint their arms, thighs, and legs with an ointment made of a thing called limons, which is a kind of fruit like small pease, and then they have no dread of cockodrills, or other venomous things. This water runs, flowing and ebbing, by a side of the mountain; and in that river men find precious stones and pearls, in great abundance. And the people of that isle say commonly, that the serpents and wild beasts of the country will do no harm to any foreigner that enters that country, but only to men that are born there.

CHAPTER XIX.

HOW MEN KNOW BY AN IDOL IF THE SICK SHALL DIE OR NOT—OF PEOPLE OF DIVERS SHAPES, AND MARVELOUSLY DISFIGURED; AND OF THE MONKS THAT GIVE THEIR RELIEF TO BABOONS, APES, MONKEYS, AND TO OTHER BEASTS.

From that isle, in going by sea toward the south, is another great isle called Dondun, in which are people of wicked kinds, so that the father eats the son, the son the father, the husband the wife, and the wife the husband. And if it so befall that the father or mother or any of their friends are sick, the son goes to the priest of their law, and prays him to ask the idol if his father or mother or friend shall die; and then the priest and the son go before the idol, and kneel full devoutly, and ask of the idol; and if the devil that is within answer that he shall live, they keep him well; and if he say that he shall die, then the priest and the son go with the wife of him that is sick, and they put their hands upon his mouth and stop his breath, and so kill him. And after that, they chop all the body in small pieces, and pray all his friends to come and eat; and they send for all the minstrels of the country and make a solemn feast. And when they have eaten the flesh, they take the bones and bury them, and sing and make great melody.

The king of this isle is a great and powerful lord, and has under his fifty-four great isles, which give tribute to him; and in every one of these isles is a king crowned, all obedient to that king. In one of these isles are people of great stature, like giants, hideous to look upon; and they have but one eye, which is in the middle of the forehead; and they eat nothing but raw flesh and fish. And in another isle toward the south dwell people of foul stature and cursed nature, who have no heads, but their eyes are in their shoulders.

In another isle are people who have the face all flat, without nose and without mouth. In another isle are people that have the lip above the mouth so great, that when they sleep in the sun they cover all the face with that lip. And in another isle there are dwarfs, which have no mouth, but instead of their mouth they have a little round hole; and when they shall eat or drink, they take it through a pipe, or a pen, or such a thing, and suck it in. And in another isle are people that have ears so long that they hang down to their knees. And in another isle are people that have horses' feet. In another isle are people that go upon their hands and feet like beasts, and are all skinned and feathered, and would leap as lightly into trees, and from tree to tree, as squirrels or apes. In another isle are hermaphrodites. And in another isle are people that go always upon their knees, and at every step they go it seems that they would fall; and they have eight toes on every foot. Many other divers people of divers natures there are in other isles about, of the which it were too long to tell.

From these isles, in passing by the Sea of Ocean toward the east, by many days, men find a great kingdom called Mancy, which is in India the Greater; and it is the best land, and one of the fairest in all the world; and the most delightful and plentiful of all goods. In that land dwell many Christians and Saracens, for it is a good and great country, and there are in it more than two thousand great and rich cities, besides other great towns. And there is greater plenty of people there than in any other part of India. In that country is no needy man; and they are very fair people, but they are all pale. And the men have thin and long beards, though with few hairs, scarcely any man having more than fifty hairs in his beard, and one hair set here, another there, as the beard of a leopard or cat. In that land are many fairer women than in any other country beyond the sea; and therefore they call that land Albany, because the people are white.

And the chief city of that country is called Latoryn; it is a day from the sea, and much larger than Paris. In that city is a great river, bearing ships, which go to all the coasts on the sea, for no city of the world is so well stored of ships. And all the inhabitants of the city and of the country worship idols. In that country the birds are twice as large as they are here. There are white geese, red about the neck, with a great crest like a cock's comb upon their heads; and they are much greater there than here. And there is great abundance of serpents, of which men make great feasts, and eat them at great solemnities. And he that maketh there a feast, be it ever so costly, unless he have serpents it is not esteemed.

There are many good cities in that country, and men have great plenty of all wines and victuals cheap. In that country are many churches of religious men of their law; and in the churches are idols as great as giants. And to these idols they give to eat, at great festival days, in this manner: they bring before them meat, hot from the fire, and they let the smoke go up toward the idols; and then they say that the idols have eaten, and then the religious men eat the meat afterward. In that country are white hens without feathers, but they bear white wool, as sheep do here. In that country, women that are unmarried carry tokens on their heads, like coronets, to be known for unmarried. Also in that country are beasts taught by men to go into waters, rivers, and deep ponds, to take fish; which beast is little, and men call them loyres. And when men cast them into the water, anon they bring up great fishes, as many as men will.

And from that city, at a distance of many days' journey, is another city, one of the greatest in the world, called Cansay, that is to say, the city of heaven. It is full fifty miles about, and is so populous that in one house men make ten households. In that city are twelve principal gates; and before each gate, three or four miles distant is a great town or city. That city is situated upon a great lake on the sea, like Venice. And in that city are more than twelve thousand bridges; and upon every bridge are strong and good towers, in which dwell the wardens to keep the city from the Great Chan. And on the one side of the city runs a great river all along the city. And there dwell Christians, and many merchants and other people of divers nations, because the land is so good and abundant. And there grows very good wine, which they call bigon, which is very strong and mild in drinking. This is a royal city, where the King of Mancy formerly resided; and there dwell many religious men, much resembling the order of friars, for they are mendicants.

From that city men go by water, solacing and disporting them, till they come to an abbey of monks fast by, who are good religious men, after their faith and law. In that abbey is a great and fair garden, where are many trees of divers kinds of fruits; and in this garden is a little hill, full of pleasant trees. In that hill and garden are various animals, as apes, monkeys, baboons, and many other divers beasts; and every day, when the monks have eaten, the almoner carries what remains to the garden and strikes on the garden gate with a silver clicket that he holds in his hand, and anon all the beasts of the hill, and of divers places of the garden, come out, to the number of three or four thousand; and they come in manner of poor men; and men give them the remnants in fair vessels of silver gilt.

And when they have eaten, the monk strikes again on the garden gate with the clicket, and all the beasts return to the places they came from. And they say that these beasts are souls of worthy men, that resemble in likeness the beasts that are fair; and therefore they give them meat for the love of God. And the other beasts, that are foul, they say, are souls of poor men; and thus they believe, and no man may put them out of this opinion. These beasts they take when they are young, and nourish them thus with alms, as many as they may find. And I asked them if it had not been better to have given that relief to poor men, rather than to the beasts. And they answered me, and said that they had no poor men amongst them in that country; and though it had been so that poor men had been among them, yet were it greater alms to give it to those souls that here do their penance. Many other marvels are in that city, and in the country thereabout, that were too long to tell you.

From that city men go by land six days to another city called Chilenfo, of which the walls are twenty miles in circumference. In that city are sixty bridges of stone, so far that no man may see fairer. In that city was the first seat of the King of Mancy, for it is a fair city and plentiful in all goods. Hence we pass across a great river called Dalay, which is the greatest river of fresh water in the world; for where it is narrowest it is more than four miles broad. And then men enter again the land of the Great Chan. The river goes through the land of pigmies, where the people are small, but three spans long; and they are right fair and gentle, both the men and the women. They live but six or seven years at most, and he that liveth eight years is considered very aged. These men are the best workers of gold, silver, cotton, silk, and of all such things, that are in the world.

And they have oftentimes war with the birds of the country, which they take and eat. This little people neither labor in lands nor in vineyards; but they have great men amongst them, of our stature, who till the land and labor amongst the vines for them. And of the men of our stature they have as great scorn and wonder as we should have among us of giants. There is a great and fair city amongst others, with a large population of the little people; and there are great men dwelling amongst them; but when they get children they are as little as pigmies; and therefore they are for the most part all pigmies, for the nature of the land is such.

From that city men go by land, by many cities and towns, to a city called Jamchay, which is noble and rich, and of great profit to the lord; and thither go men to seek all kinds of merchandise. The lord of the country hath every year, for rent of that city (as they of the city say), fifty thousand cumants of florins of gold; for they count there all by cumants, and every cumant is ten thousand florins of gold. The king of that country is very powerful, yet he is under the Great Chan, who hath under him twelve such provinces. In that country, in the good towns, is a good custom; for whoever will make a feast to any of his friends, there are certain inns in every good town; and he that will make a feast will say to the host, "Array for me, to-morrow, a good dinner for so many people," and tells him the number, and devises him the viands; and he says, also, "Thus much I will spend, and no more." And anon the host arrays for him, so fair, and so well, and so honestly, that there shall lack nothing; and it shall be done sooner, and with less cost, than if it were done in his own house.

Five miles from that city, toward the head of the river of Dalay, is another city, called Menke, in which is a strong navy of ships, all white as snow, from the color of the trees of which they are made; and they are very great and fair ships, and well ordained, and made with halls and chambers, and other casements, as though it were on land. From thence men go by many towns and many cities to a city called Lanteryne, eight days from the city last mentioned. This city is situated upon a fair, great, and broad river, called Caramaron, which passes through Cathay; and it often overflows and does much harm.

CHAPTER XX.

OF THE GREAT CHAN OF CATHAY—OF THE ROYALTY OF HIS PALACE, AND HOW HE SITS AT MEAT; AND OF THE GREAT NUMBER OF OFFICERS THAT SERVE HIM.

CATHAY is a great country, fair, noble, rich, and full of merchants. Thither merchants go to seek spices and all manner of merchandises, more commonly than in any other part. And you shall understand that merchants who come from Genoa, or from Venice, or from Romania, or other parts of Lombardy, go by sea and by land eleven or twelve months, or more sometimes before they reach the Isle of Cathay, which is the principal region of all parts beyond; and it belongs to the Great Chan. From Cathay men go toward the east, by many days' journey, to a good city, between these others, called Sugarmago, one of the best stored with silk and other merchandises in the world.

Then men come to another old city, toward the east in the province of Cathay, near which the men of Tartary have made another city, called Caydon, which has twelve gates. And between the two gates there is always a great mile; so that the two cities, that is to say the old and the new, have in circuit more than twenty miles. In this city is the seat of the Great Chan, in a very great palace, the fairest in the world, the walls of which are in circuit more than two miles; and within the walls it is all full of other palaces. And in the garden of the great palace there is a great hill, upon which there is another palace, the fairest and richest that any man may devise. And all about the palace and the hill are many trees bearing divers fruits. And all about that hill are great and deep ditches; and beside them are great fish-ponds, on both sides; and there is a very fair bridge to pass over the ditches. And in these fish-ponds are an extraordinary number of wild geese and ganders, and wild ducks, and swans, and herons. And all about these ditches and fish-ponds is the great garden, full of wild beasts, so that, when the Great Chan will have any sport, to take any of the wild beasts, or of the fowls, he will cause them to be driven, and take them at the windows, without going out of his chamber.

Within the palace, in the hall, there are twenty-four pillars of fine gold; and all the walls are covered within with red skins of animals called panthers, fair beasts and well smelling; so that, for the sweet odor of the skins, no evil air may enter into the palace. The skins are as red as blood, and shine so bright against the sun that a man may scarcely look at them. And many people worship the beasts when they meet them first in a morning, for their great virtue and for the good smell that they have; and the skins they value more than if they were plates of fine gold. And in the middle of this palace is the mountour of the Great Chan, all wrought of gold and of precious stones, and great pearls; and at the four corners are four serpents of gold; and all about there are made large nets of silk and gold, and great pearls hanging all about it. And under the mountour are conduits of beverage that they drink in the emperor's court. And beside the conduits are many vessels of gold, with which they that are of the household drink at the conduit.

The hall of the palace is full nobly arrayed, and full marvelously attired on all parts, in all things that men apparel any hall with. And first, at the head of the hall, is the emperor's throne, very high, where he sits at meat. It is of fine precious stones, bordered all about with purified gold and precious stones, and great pearls. And the steps up to the table are of precious stones mixed with gold. And at the left side of the emperor's seat is the seat of his first wife, one step lower than the emperor, and it is of jasper, bordered with gold and precious stones. And the seat of his second wife is lower than his first wife; and is also of jasper, bordered with gold, as that other is And the seat of the third wife is still lower, by a step, than the second wife; for he has always three wives with him, wherever he is. And after his wives, on the same side, sit the ladies of his lineage, still lower, according to their ranks. And all those that are married have a counterfeit, made like a man's foot, upon their heads, a cubit long, all wrought with great, fine, and orient pearls, and above made with peacocks' feathers, and of other shining feathers; and that stands upon their heads like a crest, in token that they are under man's foot, and under subjection of man. And they that are unmarried have none such.

And after, at the right side of the emperor, first sits his eldest son, who shall reign after him, one step lower than the emperor, in such manner of seats as do the empresses; and after him other great lords of his lineage, each of them a step lower than the other, according to their rank. The emperor has his table alone by himself, which is of gold and precious stones; or of crystal, bordered with gold and full of precious stones; or of amethysts, or of lignum aloes, that comes out of Paradise; or of ivory, bound or bordered with gold. And each of his wives has also her table by herself. And his eldest son, and the other lords also, and the ladies, and all that sit with the emperor, have very rich tables, alone by themselves. And under the emperor's table sit four clerks, who write all that the emperor says, be it good or evil; for all that he says must be held good; for he may not change his word nor revoke it.

At great feasts, men bring, before the emperor's table, great tables of gold, and thereon are peacocks of gold, and many other kinds of different fowls, all of gold, and richly wrought and enameled; and they make them dance and sing, clapping their wings together, and making great noise; and whether it be by craft or by necromancy I know not, but it is a goodly sight to behold. But I have the less marvel, because they are the most skillful men in the world in all sciences and in all crafts; for in subtilty, malice, and forethought they surpass all men under heaven; and therefore they say themselves that they see with two eyes, and the Christians see but with one, because they are more subtle than they. I busied myself much to learn that craft; but the master told me that he had made a vow to his god to teach it no creature, but only to his eldest son.

Also above the emperor's table and the other tables, and above a great part of the hall, is a vine made of fine gold, which spreads all about the hall; and it has many clusters of grapes, some white, some green, some yellow, some red, and some black, all of precious stones; the white are of crystal, beryl, and iris; the yellow, of topazes; the red, of rubins, grenaz, and alabraundines; the green of emeralds, of perydoz, and of chrysolites; and the black of onyx and garnets. And they are all so properly made, that it appears a real vine, bearing natural grapes. And before the emperor's table stand great lords and rich barons, and others that serve the emperor at meat; and no man is so bold as to speak a word, unless the emperor speak to him, except minstrels, that sing songs and tell jests or other disports to solace the emperor.

And all the vessels that men are served with, in the hall or in chambers, are of precious stones, and especially at great tables, either of jasper, or of crystal, or of amethyst, or of fine gold. And the cups are of emeralds, and sapphires, or topazes, of perydoz, and of many other precious stones. Vessel of silver is there none, for they set no value on it to make vessels of; but they make therewith steps, and pillars, and pavements, to halls and chambers. And before the hall door stand many barons and knights full armed, to hinder any one from entering, unless by the will or command of the emperor, except they be servants or minstrels of the household.

And you shall understand that my fellows and I, with our yeomen, served this emperor, and were his soldiers, fifteen months, against the King of Mancy, who was at war with him, because we had great desire to see his nobleness, and the estate of his court, and all his government, to know if it were such as we heard say. And truly we found it more noble, and more excellent and rich, and more marvelous, than ever we heard, insomuch that we would never have believed it had we not seen it. For it is not there as it is here. For the lords here have a certain number of people as they may suffice; but the Great Chan hath every day people at his cost and expense without number. But the ordinance, nor the expenses in meat and drink, nor the honesty, nor the cleanliness, is not so arranged there as it is here; for all the commons there eat without cloth upon their knees; and they eat all manner of flesh, and little of bread.

And after meat they wipe their hands upon their skirts, and they eat but once a day. But the estate of lords is full great, and rich, and noble. And although some men will not believe me, but hold it for fable, to tell them the nobleness of his person, and of his estate, and of his court, and of the great multitude of people that he has, nevertheless I will tell you a little of him and of his people, according as I have seen the manner and order full many a time; and whoever will may believe me, if he will, and whoever will not, may choose.

CHAPTER XXI.

WHEREFORE HE IS CALLED THE GREAT CHAN—OF THE STYLE OF HIS LETTERS; AND OF THE SUPERSCRIPTION ABOUT HIS GREAT SEAL AND HIS PRIVY SEAL.

First I shall tell you why he was called the Great Chan. You shall understand that all the world was destroyed by Noah's flood, except only Noah, and his wife, and his children. Noah had three sons, Shem, Cham (*i.e.* Ham), and Japheth. This Cham was he who saw his father naked when he slept, and showed him to his brethren in scorn, and therefore he was cursed of God. And Japheth turned his face away, and covered him. These three brethren shared all the land; and this Cham, for his cruelty, took the greater and the best part, toward the east, which is called Asia; and Shem took Africa; and Japheth took Europe; and therefore is all the earth parted in these three parts, by these three brethren. Cham was the greatest and most mighty; and of him came more generations than of the others. And of his son Cush was engendered Nimrod the giant, who was the first king that ever was in the world, and he began the foundation of the Tower of Babylon.

And that time the fiends of hell came many times and lay with the women of his generation, and engendered on them divers people, as monsters, and people disfigured, some without heads, some with great ears, some with one eye, some giants, some with horse's feet, and many other different shapes contrary to nature. And of that generation of Cham are come the pagans, and different people that are in islands of the sea about India. And forasmuch as he was the most mighty, and no man might withstand him, he called himself the son of God, and sovereign of all the world. And on account of this Cham, this emperor called himself Chan and sovereign of all the world. And of the generation of Shem are come the Saracens: And of the generation of Japheth came the people of Israel. And though we dwell in Europe, this is the opinion that the Syrians and the Samaritans have amongst them, and that they told me before I went toward India; but I found it otherwise.

Nevertheless the truth is this—that Tartars, and they that dwell in Greater Asia, came of Cham. But the Emperor of Cathay was called not Cham, but Chan; and I shall tell you how. It is but little more than eight-score years since Tartary was in subjection and servage to other nations about; for they were but herdsmen, and did nothing but keep beasts, and lead them to pastures. But among them they had seven principal nations that were sovereigns of them all, of which the first nation or lineage was called Tartar; and that is the most noble and the most praised. The second lineage is called Tanghot; the third, Eurache; the fourth, Valair; the fifth, Semoche; the sixth, Megly; the seventh, Coboghe. Now it befell that of the first lineage succeeded an old worthy man, that was not rich, who was called Changuys. This man lay one night in bed, and he saw in a vision that there came before him a knight armed all in white, and he sat upon a white horse, and said to him, "Chan, sleepest thou? The immortal God hath sent me to thee; and it is His will that thou go to the seven lineages, and say to them that thou shalt be their emperor; for thou shalt conquer the lands and the countries that are about; and they that march upon you shall be under your subjection, as you have been under theirs; for that is God's immortal will."

Changuys arose, and went to the seven lineages, and told them what the white knight had said. And they scorned him, and said that he was a fool; and so he departed from them all ashamed. And the night following this white knight came to the seven lineages, and commanded them, on behalf of the immortal God, that they should make this Changuys their emperor, and they should be out of subjection, and they should·hold all other regions about them in servage, as they had been to them before. And next day they chose him to be their emperor, and set him upon a black chest, and after that lifted him up with great solemnity, and set him in a chair of gold, and did him all manner of reverence; and they called him Chan, as the white knight called him. And when he was thus chosen, he would make trial if he might trust in them or not, and whether they would be obedient to him, and then he made many statutes and ordinances, that they call *Ysya Chan*.

The first statute was, that they should believe in and obey immortal God, who is almighty, and who would cast them out of servage, and they should at all times call to Him for help in time of need. The second statute was, that all manner of men that might bear arms should be numbered, and to every ten should be a master, and to every hundred a master, and to every thousand a master, and to every ten thousand a master. After, he commanded the principals of the seven lineages to leave and forsake all they had in goods and heritage, and from thenceforth to be satisfied with what he would give them of his grace. And they did so immediately. After this he commanded the principals of the seven lineages, that each should bring his eldest son before him, and with their own hands smite off their heads without delay. And immediately his command was performed.

And when the Chan saw that they made no obstacle to perform his commandment, then he thought that he might well trust in them, and he commanded them presently to make them ready, and to follow his banner. And after this the Chan put in subjection all the lands about him. Afterward it befell on a day that the Chan rode with a few companies to behold the strength of the country that he had won, and a great multitude of his enemies met with him, and to give good example of bravery to his people, he was the first that fought, and rushed into the midst of his enemies, and there was thrown from his horse, and his horse slain. And when his people saw him on the earth, they were all discouraged, and thought he had been dead, and fled every one; and their enemies pursued them, but they knew not that the emperor was there. And when they were returned from the pursuit they sought the woods, if any of them had been hid in them; and many they found and slew.

So it happened that as they went searching toward the place where the emperor was they saw an owl sitting on a tree above him; and then they said amongst them that there was no man there, because they saw the bird there, and so they went their way; and thus the emperor escaped death. And then he went secretly by night, till he came to his people, who were very glad of his coming, and gave great thanks to immortal God, and to that bird by which their lord was saved; and therefore, above all fowls of the world, they worship the owl; and when they have any of its feathers, they keep them full preciously, intead of relics, and bear them upon their heads with great reverence; and they hold themselves blessed, and safe from all perils, while they have these feathers on them, and therefore they bear them upon their heads. After all this the Chan assembled all his people, and went against those who had assailed him before, and destroyed them, and put them in subjection and servage.

And when he had won and put all the lands and countries on this side Mount Belian in subjection, the white knight came to him again in his sleep, and said to him, " Chan, the will of immortal God is, that thou pass Mount Belian; and thou shalt win the land, and thou shalt put many nations in subjection; and because thou shalt find no good passage to go toward that country, go to Mount Belian, which is upon the sea, and kneel there nine times toward the east, in the worship of immortal God, and He shall show the way to pass by." And the Chan did so. And soon the sea, that touched and was close to the mountain, began to withdraw itself, and exhibited a fair way of nine feet broad; and so he passed with his people, and won the land of Cathay, which is the greatest kingdom in the world. And on account of the nine kneelings, and the nine feet of way, the Chan and all the men of Tartary have the number nine in great reverence. And, therefore, he that will make the Chan any present, be it horses, birds, arrows, bows, or fruit, or any other thing, he must always make it of the number nine; and so the presents are more agreeable to him, and better received, than if he were presented with a hundred or two hundred.

Also, when the Chan of Cathay had won the country of Cathay, and put in subjection many countries about, he fell sick. And when he felt that he should die, he said to his twelve sons, that each of them should bring him one of his arrows, and so they did anon. And then he commanded that they should bind them together in three places, and then he gave them to his eldest son, and bade him break them; and he exerted himself with all his might to break them, but he might not. And then the Chan bade his second son break them, and so to the others one after another; but none of them might break them. And then he bade the youngest son separate them from each other, and break every one by itself, and so he did. And then said the Chan to his eldest son, and to all the others, "Wherefore might you not break them?" And they answered that they might not, because they were bound together. "And wherefore," quoth he, "hath your little youngest brother broke them?" "Because," quoth they, "they were separated from each other." Then said the Chan, "My sons, truly thus will it fare with you; for as long as you are bound together in three places, that is to say, in love, truth, and good accord, no man shall have power to grieve you; but if you be divided from these three places, that one of you help not the other, you shall be destroyed and brought to nothing; and if each of you love each other, and help each other, you shall be lords and sovereigns over all other people.'

And when he had made his ordinances he died; and then, after him, reigned Ecchecha Chan, his eldest son. And his other brethren went to subdue many countries and kingdoms, unto the land of Prussia and Russia, and took the name of Chans, but they were all subject to their eldest brother, and therefore was he called Great Chan. After Ecchecha reigned Guyo Chan, and after him Mango

Chan, who was a good Christian man, and baptized and gave letters of perpetual peace to all Christian men and sent his brother Halaon, with a great multitude of people, to win the Holy Land, and put it into the hands of the Christians, and destroy the law of Mohammed, and take the Caliph of Bagdad, who was emperor and lord of all the Saracens.

And when this Caliph was taken they found him so rich in treasure, and of so high worship, that in all the rest of the world no man might find a man higher in worship. And then Halaon made him come before him, and said to him, "Why hadst thou not hired with thee more soldiers for a little quantity of treasure, to defend thee and thy country, who art so abundant of treasure and so high in all worship?" And the Caliph answered, that he believed he had enough of his own proper men. And then said Halaon, "Thou wert as a god of the Saracens; and it is convenient to a god to eat no meat that is mortal; and, therefore, thou shalt eat only precious stones, rich pearls, and treasure that thou lovest so much." And then he ordered him to prison, and placed all his treasure about him; and so he died for hunger and thirst. And then after this Halaon won all the Land of Promise, and put it into the hands of the Christians. But the Great Chan, his brother, died, and that was great sorrow and loss to all Christians. After Mango Chan reigned Cobyla Chan, who was also a Christian, and reigned forty-two years. He founded the great city Igonge in Cathay, which is much larger than Rome. The other Great Chan who came after him, became a pagan, and all the others since.

The kingdom of Cathay is the greatest realm in the world; and the Great Chan is the most powerful emperor and greatest lord under the firmament; and so he calls himself in his letters right thus, "Chan, son of the high God, emperor of all who inhabit the earth, and lord of all lords." And the letter of his great seal has the inscription, "God in heaven, Chan upon the earth, his fortitude; the seal of the emperor of all men." And the superscription about his little seal is this: "The fortitude of God; the seal of the emperor of all men." And although they are not christened, yet the emperor and all the Tartars believe in immortal God; and when they will threaten any man, they say, "God knoweth well that I shall do thee such a thing," and tell their menace.

CHAPTER XXII.

OF THE GOVERNMENT OF THE GREAT CHAN'S COURT, AND WHEN HE MAKES SOLEMN FEASTS—OF HIS PHILOSOPHERS; AND OF HIS ARRAY WHEN HE RIDES ABROAD.

Now shall I tell you the government of the court of the Great Chan, when he makes solemn feasts, which is principally four times in the year. The first feast is of his birth; the second is of his presentation in their temple, such as they call here moseache (mosque), where they make a kind of circumcision; and the other two feasts are of his idols. The first feast of the idol is when he is first put into their temple and throned. The other feast is when the idol begins first to speak or work miracles. There are no more solemn feasts, except when he marries one of his children. At each of these feasts he hath great multitudes of people, well ordained and well arrayed, by thousands, by hundreds, and by tens. Every man knoweth well what service he shall do; and every man gives so good heed and so good attendance to his service that no man finds any fault.

There are first appointed four thousand barons, mighty and rich, to govern and make ordinance for the feast, and to serve the emperor. And these solemn feasts are held in halls and tents made full nobly of cloths of gold and of tartaries. All the barons have crowns of gold upon their heads, very noble and rich, full of precious stones and great orient pearls. And they are all clothed in clothes of gold, or of tartaries, or of camakas, so richly and perfectly, that no man in the world can amend it or devise better; and all these robes are embroidered with gold all about, and dubbed full of precious stones and of great orient pearls, full richly. And they may well do so, for cloths of gold and of silk are cheaper there by much than are cloths of wool.

These four thousand barons are divided into four companies, and every thousand is clothed in cloths all of one color, and so well arrayed and so richly, that it is marvel to behold. The first thousand, which is of dukes, earls, marquises, and admirals, all in cloths of gold, with tissues of green silk, and bordered with gold, full of precious stones. The second thousand is all in cloths diapered of red silk, all wrought with gold, and the orfrayes set full of great pearls and precious stones, full nobly wrought. The third thou-

sand is clothed in cloths of silk, of purple, or of India. And the
fourth thousand is in clothes of yellow. And all their clothes are
so nobly and richly wrought with gold and precious stones and rich
pearls, that if a man of this country had but one of their robes, he
might well say that he should never be poor. For the gold and the
precious stones, and the great orient pearls, are of greater value on
this side the sea than in those countries.

And when they are thus appareled they go two and two together,
full orderly, before the emperor, without uttering a word, only
bowing to him. And each of them carries a tablet of jasper, or
ivory, or crystal; and the minstrels go before them, sounding their
instruments of divers melody. When the first thousand is thus
passed, and hath made its muster, it withdraws on the one side; and
then enters the second thousand, and proceeds in the same manner
of array and countenance as the first; and so the third, and then
the fourth, and none of them utters a word.

And at one side of the emperor's table sit many philosophers,
who are proved for wise men in many divers sciences, as in astronomy, necromancy, geomancy, pyromancy, hydromancy, augury,
and many other sciences. And each of them has before him, some
astrolabes of gold, some spheres, some the skull of a dead man,
some vessels of gold full of gravel or sand, some vessels of gold full
of burning coals, some vessels of gold full of water, wine, and oil,
and some horloges (clocks) of gold, made full nobly and richly
wrought, and many other sorts of instruments after their sciences.
And at certain hours they say to certain officers who stand before
them, appointed for the time to fulfill their command, "Make
peace." And then the officers say, "Now peace, listen." And
after that another of the philosophers says, "Every man do reverence, and bow to the emperor, who is God's son and sovereign lord
of all the world; for now is time." And then every man bows his
head toward the earth. And then the same philosopher commands
again, "Stand up." And they do so And at another hour another philosopher says, "Put your little finger in your ears." And
anon they do so. And at another hour another philosopher says,
"Put your hand before your mouth." And anon they do so And
at another hour another philosopher says, "Put your hand upon
your head." And after that he biddeth them to take their hand
away, and they do so.

And so, from hour to hour, they command certain things. And
they say that those things have divers significations. I asked
them privately what those things betokened. And one of the

masters told me that the bowing of the head at that hour betokened that all those that bowed their heads should ever more after be obedient and true to the emperor. And the putting of the little finger in the ear betokens, as they say, that none of them shall hear anything spoken contradictory to the emperor, without telling it anon to his council, or discovering it to some men that will make relation to the emperor. And so forth of all other things done by the philosophers. And no man performs any duty to the emperor, either clothing, or bread, or wine, or bath, or other thing that belongeth to him, but at certain hours, as his philosophers devise well.

And if there fall war, anon the philosophers come and give their advice after their calculations, and counsel the emperor by their sciences; so that the emperor does nothing without their council. And when the philosophers have done and performed their commands, then the minstrels begin to do their minstrelsy on their different instruments, each after the other, with all the melody they can devise. And when they have performed a good while, one of the officers of the emperor goes up on a high stage, wrought full curiously, and cries and says with a loud voice, " Make peace." And then every man is still. And then, anon after, all the lords of the emperor's lineage, nobly arrayed in rich cloths of gold, and royally apparelled on white steeds, as many as may well follow him at that time, are ready to make their presents to the emperor. And then says the steward of the court to the lords, by name, " N. of N.," and names first the most noble and the worthiest by name, and says, " Be ye ready with such a number of white horses to serve the emperor your sovereign." And, to another lord, he says, " N. of N., be ye ready with such a number to serve your sovereign lord." And to another, right so. And to all the lords of the emperor's lineage, one after the other, as they are of estate.

And when they are all called they enter one after the other, and present the white horses to the emperor, and then go their way. And then, all the other barons, one by one, give him presents, or jewels, or some other thing, according to their rank. And then, after them, all the prelates of their law, and religious men and others; and every man gives him something. And when all men have thus offered to the emperor, the greatest dignitary of the prelates gives him a blessing, saying an orison of their law. And then begin the minstrels to make their minstrelsy on divers instruments, with all the melody that they can devise.

When they have done their craft, then they bring in before the emperor lions, leopards, and other divers beasts, and eagles, and vultures, and other divers fowls, and fishes, and serpents, to do him reverence. And then come jugglers and enchanters that do many marvels; for they cause the sun and the moon to come in the air, apparently, to every man's sight. And afterward they make the night so dark that no man may see. And after that they make the day to come again, fair and pleasant, with bright sun, to every man's sight. And then they bring in dancers of the fairest damsels in the world, and most richly arrayed.

Next they cause to come in other damsels bringing cups of gold full of milk of divers beasts, who give drink to lords and to ladies. And then they make knights to joust in arms full lustily; and they run together and fight full fiercely; and they break their spears so rudely that the fragments fly in pieces all about the hall. And then they cause to come in hunting for the hart and for the boar, with hounds running with open mouth. And many other things they do by craft of their enchantments, which it is marvelous to see. And such plays of sport they make, until the taking up of the boards.

This Great Chan hath a vast multitude of people to serve him, as I have told you before For he hath of minstrels the number of thirteen cumants, but they abide not always with him. For all the minstrels that come before him, of whatever nation they are are retained with him, as of his household, and entered in his books as for his own men. And after that, wherever they go, evermore they rank as minstrels of the Great Chan; and, under that title, all kings and lords cherish them the more with gifts and all things. And therefore he hath so great multitude of them. And he hath of certain men, as though they were yeomen, that keep birds as ostriches, gerfalcons, sparrow-hawks, gentle falcons, lanyers, sacres, sacrettes, well-speaking parrots, and singing birds, and also of wild beasts, as of elephants, tame and others, baboons, apes, monkeys, and other divers beasts, to the number of fifteen cumants of yeomen.

And of Christian physicians he has two hundred; and of leeches that are Christians he has two hundred and ten; and of leeches and physicians that are Saracens, twenty; for he trusts more in the Christian leeches than in the Saracens. And his other common household is without number: all having all necessaries from the emperor's court. And he has in his court many barons, as servitors, that are Christians, and converted to good faith by the preaching of religious Christian men who dwell with him, and there are many that will not have it known that they are Christians.

This emperor may spend as much as he will, without estimation, for his only money is of leather imprinted, or of paper, of which some is of greater price and some of less, after the diversity of his statutes. And when that money has run so long that it begins to waste, men carry it to the emperor's treasury, and receive new money for the old. And that money passes throughout the country. For there, and beyond them, they make no money of gold or silver. Therefore, he may spend very largely. And of gold and silver that men have in this country, he makes ceilings, pillars, and pavements in his palace, and other divers things. This emperor hath in his chamber, in one of the pillars of gold, a ruby and a carbuncle of half a foot long, which in the night gives so great light and shining, that it is as light as day. And he hath many other precious stones, and many other rubies and carbuncles, but those are the greatest and most precious.

This emperor dwells in summer in a city toward the north, called Saduz, where it is cold; and in winter he dwells in a city called Camaaleche, in a hot country. But the country where he dwells most commonly is in Gaydo, or in Jong, a good and temperate country after the weather that is there; but to men of our part of the world, it is excessively hot. And when this emperor will ride from one country to another, he appoints four hosts of his people, of the which the first host goes before him a day's journey, for that host shall be lodged the night where the emperor shall lie upon the morrow. And there shall every man have all manner of victuals and necessaries at the emperor's cost.

And in this first host the number of people is fifty cumants of horse and foot, of which every cumant amounts to ten thousand, as I have told you before. And another host goes on the right side of the emperor, nigh half a day's journey from him; and another goes on the left side of him in the same manner. And in every host is the same number of people. Then after comes the fourth host, which is much greater than any of the other, and goes behind him, the distance of a bow's draught. And every host has its day's journey ordained in certain places, where they shall be lodged at night, and there they shall have all they need. And if it befall that one of the host die, anon they put another in his place, so that the number shall ever be complete.

And you shall understand that the emperor, in person, rides not as other great lords do, unless he choose to go privately with few men, to be unknown. Otherwise, he sits in a chariot with four wheels, upon which is made a fair chamber; and it is made of a certain wood that comes out of terrestrial paradise, which they call lignum aloes. And this chamber is full well smelling, because of the wood it is made of; and it is all covered internally with plates of fine gold, dubbed with precious stones and great pearls. And four elephants and four great steeds, all white and covered with rich coverings, draw the chariot. And four, or five, or six of the greatest lords ride about this chariot, full richly and nobly arrayed, so that no man shall approach the chariot except those lords, unless the emperor call any man to him that he wishes to speak with. And above the chamber of this chariot in which the emperor sits, are set upon a perch, four, five, or six gerfalcons, to that intent, that when the emperor sees any wild fowl, he may take it at his own list, and have the sport, first with one and then with another; and so he takes his sport passing through the country.

And no man of his company rides before him, but all after him. And no man dare approach within a bow-shot of the chariot, except those lords only that are about him, and all the host come fairly after him, in great multitude. And also such another chariot, with such hosts, ordained and arrayed, go with the empress upon another side, each by itself, with four hosts, right as the emperor did, but not with so great multitude of people. And his eldest son goes by another way in another chariot, in the same manner. So that there is between them so great multitude of folks that it is marvelous to tell it. And sometimes it happens that when he will not go far, and he chooses to have the empress and his children with him, that they go all together; and then the people are mixed in one company and divided in four parts only.

The empire of this Great Chan is divided into twelve provinces; and every province has more than two thousand cities, and towns without number. This country is very extensive, for it has twelve principal kings in twelve provinces; and each of those kings has many kings under him; and they are all subject to the Great Chan. And his land and lordship extends so far that a man may not go from one end to the other, either by sea or land, in less than seven years. And through the deserts of his lordship, where are no towns, there are inns appointed at every day's journey, to receive both man and horse, in which they shall find plenty of victuals and all things they need in their way.

And there is a marvelous, but profitable, custom in that country, that if there happen any contrary thing that should be prejudicial or grievous to the emperor, in any kind, anon the emperor has tidings thereof and full knowledge in a day, though it be three or four days from him, or more. For his envoys take their dromedaries, or their horses, and they ride as fast as they may toward one of the inns; and when they come there they blow a horn, and anon they of the inn know that there are tidings to warn the emperor of some rebellion against him; and they make other men ready, in all haste that they may, to carry letters, and ride as fast as they may, till they come to the other inns with their letters; and then they make fresh men ready, to ride forth with the letters toward the emperor, while the last bringer rests himself, and baits his dromedary or horse; and so from inn to inn, till it comes to the emperor. And thus anon he has quick tidings of anything by his couriers, that run so hastliy through all the country.

And, also, when the emperor sends his couriers in haste throughout his land, each of them has a large thong full of small bells; and when they approach the inns of other couriers, they ring their bells; and anon the other couriers make them ready, and run their way to another inn; and thus one runs to another, full speedily and swiftly, till the emperor's intent be served in all haste. And these couriers are called *chydydo*, after their language, that is to say, a messenger.

Also when the emperor goes from one country to another, as I have told you before, and he passes through cities and towns, every man makes a fire before his door, and puts therein powder of good gums, that are sweet smelling, to make good savor to the emperor; and all the people kneel down toward him, and do him great reverence. And there, where Christian monks dwell, as they do in many cities in the land, they go before him in procession, with cross and holy water; and they sing *Veni creator spiritus*, with a high voice, and go toward him. And when he hears them, he commands his lords to ride beside him, that the religious men may come to him; and when they are nigh him with the cross, then he puts down his galiot, which is placed on his head in the manner of a chaplet, made of gold, and precious stones, and great pearls; and it is so rich that men esteem it the value of a realm in that country; and then he kneels to the cross. And then the prelate of the monks says before him certain orisons, and gives him a blessing with the cross; and he bows to the blessing full devoutly. And then the prelate gives him some sort of fruit, to the number of nine, in a plate of silver; and he takes one; and then men give to the other lords that are about him; for the custom is such that no stranger shall come before him unless he give him some manner of thing, after the old law, that says, *Nemo accedat in conspectu meo vacuus*. And then the emperor tells the monks to withdraw themselves again, that they be not hurt by the great multitude of horses that come behind him. And also in the same manner do the monks that dwell there to the empresses that pass by them, and to his eldest son; and to all of them they present fruit.

And you shall understand that this multitude of people dwell not continually with him, but are sent for when he wants them; and after, when they have done, they return to their own households, except those that are dwelling with him in the household to serve him, and his wives and sons. And although the others are departed from him after they have performed their service, yet there remain continually with him in court fifty thousand horsemen, and twenty thousand footmen, besides minstrels and those who keep wild beasts and birds There is not, under the firmament, so great a lord, nor so mighty, nor so rich, as the Great Chan; neither Prester John, who is Emperor of Upper India, nor the Sultan of Babylon, nor the Emperor of Persia

All these, in comparison to the Great Chan, are neither of might, nobleness, royalty, nor riches, for in all these he surpasses all earthly princes. Wherefore it is great harm that he believes not faithfully in God And, nevertheless, he will gladly hear speak of God, and he willingly allows Christian men to dwell in his lordship, and men of his faith to be made Christian men, if they will, throughout all his country, for he forbids no man to hold any faith but what he likes

In that country some men have one hundred wives, some sixty, some more, and some less. And they take the next of their kin to wife, excepting only their mothers, daughters, and sisters on the mother's side; but their sisters on the father's side. of another woman, they may take and their brothers' wives, also, after their death; and their step-mothers also in the same way.

CHAPTER XXIII.

OF THE LAW AND CUSTOMS OF THE TARTARS IN CATHAY; AND HOW MEN DO WHEN THE EMPEROR SHALL DIE, AND HOW HE SHALL BE CHOSEN.

The people of that country use all long clothes, without furs; and they are clothed with precious cloths of Tartary, and cloths of gold. And their clothes are slit at the side, and fastened with silk lace; and they clothe them also with pilches, the hide outside. And they use neither cap nor hood. And the women go in the same dress as the men; so that we can hardly distinguish the men from the women, except only that the women that are married bear upon their heads the token of a man's foot, in sign that they are under man's foot, and under the subjection of man. And their wives dwell not together, but each of them by herself; and the husband may lie with which of them he likes. Each has a separate house, both man and woman; and their houses are made round with staves, with a round window above, which gives them light, and also serves for the escape of smoke. And the roofing of their houses, and the walls, and the doors, are all of wood.

When they go to war, they take their houses with them upon chariots, as men do tents or pavilions. They make their fires in the middle of their houses And they have a great multitude of all manner of beasts, except swine. which they do not breed. And they believe in one God, who made and formed all things; yet they have idols of gold and silver, and of wood and of cloth, to which they offer always the first milk of their beasts, and also of their meats and drinks before they eat. And they frequently offer horses and beasts. They call the god of nature Yroga. Their emperor, whatever name he has, they add always to it Chan; and, when I was there, their emperor's name was Thiaut, so that he was called Thiaut Chan; and his eldest son was called Tossue; and when he shall be emperor, he shall be called Tossue Chan. And at that time the emperor had twelve other sons, named Cuncy, Ordii, Chahaday, Buryn, Negu, Nocab, Cadu, Siban, Cuten, Balacy, Babylan, and Garegan. And of his three wives, the first and the principal, who was Prester John's daughter, was named Serioche Chan; and the other Borak Chan; and the other Karanke Chan.

The people of that country begin all undertakings in the new moon; and they worship much the moon and the sun, and often kneel toward them. All the people of the country ride commonly without spurs; but they carry always a little whip in their hands to urge their horses. And they hold it for a great sin to cast a knife in the fire, and to draw flesh out of a pot with a knife, and to smite a horse with the handle of a whip, or to smite a horse with a bridle, or to break one bone with another, or to cast milk or any liquor that men may drink upon the earth, or to take and slay little children.

And of every one of these sins they must be shriven by their priests, and pay a great sum of silver for their penance. The place they have thus defiled must be purified before any one dare to enter it. And when they have paid their penance, men make them pass through a fire, or through two, to cleanse them of their sins. And also when any messenger comes and brings letters, or any present, to the emperor, he must pass, with the thing that he brings, through two burning fires, to purge them, that he bring no poison nor venom, nor any wicked thing, that might be grievance to the lord. And also, if any man or woman be taken in adultery or fornication, anon they slay them.

The people of that country are all good archers, and shoot right well, both men and women, as well on horseback, riding, as on foot, running. And the women do all things, and exercise all manner of trades and crafts, as of clothes, boots, and other things; and they drive carts, plows, wagons, and chariots; and make houses, and all manner of things, except bows and arrows, and armor, which are made by men. And all the women wear breeches, as well as men. All the people of that country are very obedient to their sovereign, and fight not nor chide with one another. And there are neither thieves nor robbers in that country, but every man respects the other; but no man there doth reverence to strangers, except they are great princes.

And they eat dogs, lions, leopards, mares and foals, asses, rats, and mice; and all kinds of beasts, great and small, except only swine, and beasts that were forbidden by the old law. They eat but little bread, except in courts of great lords; and they have not, in many places, either pease or beans, nor any other pottage but the broth of the flesh; for they eat little else but flesh and the broth. And when they have eaten they wipe their hands upon their skirts; for they use no napkins or towels, except before great lords. And when they have eaten, they put their dishes, unwashed, into the pot or caldron, with the remnant of the flesh and broth, till they eat again. The rich men drink milk of mares, or camels, or of asses, or other beasts. And they are easily made drunk with milk, or with another drink made of honey and water sodden together; for in that country is neither wine nor ale. They live full wretchedly, and eat but once in the day, and that but little, either in courts or other places. Indeed one man alone, in our country, will eat more in a day than they will eat in three. And if any foreign messenger come there to a lord, men make him to eat but once a day, and that very little.

When they make war they proceed with great prudence, and always do their best to destroy their enemies. Every man there bears two or three bows, and great plenty of arrows, and a great ax; and the gentlemen have short and large spears, very sharp on the one side; and they have plates and helmets made of cuirbouilli; and their horses' coverings are of the same. And whoever flies from battle they slay him. And when they hold a siege about a castle or town, which is walled and defensible, they promise them that are within to do all the profit and good, that it is marvelous to hear; and they grant also to them that are within all that they will ask them; and after they have surrendered, they slay them all, and cut off their ears, and pickle them in vinegar, and thereof make great service for lords. All their desire, and all their imagination, is to reduce all countries under their subjection; and they say that they knew well, by their prophecies, that they shall be overcome by archers; but they know not of what nation, nor of what law, they shall be who shall overcome them.

When they will make their idols, or any image of any one of their friends, to have remembrance of him, they always make the image naked, without any kind of clothing; for they say that in good love there should be no covering, that man should not love for the fair clothing, nor for the rich array, but only for the body such as God hath made it.

And you shall understand that it is very perilous to pursue the Tartars when they fly in battle; for in flying they shoot behind them, and slay both men and horses. And when they fight, they close together in a body, so that if there be twenty thousand men, you would not think there were ten thousand. They can conquer land of strangers, but they can not keep it; for they like better to lie in tents without, than in castles or in towns. They despise all other people. Amongst them oil of olives is very dear; for they hold it for a very noble medicine. All the Tartars have small eyes and little beard, and a paucity of hair. They are false and traitorous, never keeping their promises. They are a very hardy people, and able to endure much labor, more than any other people; for they are accustomed thereto in their own country from youth.

And when any man shall die they set a spear beside him; and when he draws toward death every man flies out of the house till he is dead; and after that they bury him in the fields. And when the emperor dies, they place him in a chair in the center of his tent, with a clean table before him, covered with a cloth, and thereon flesh and divers viands, and a cup full of mare's milk. And men put a mare beside him, with her foal, and a horse saddled and bridled; and they lay upon the horse great quantities of gold and silver, and they put about him great plenty of straw, and they make a great and large pit, and, with the tent and all these other things, they put him in the earth; and they say that when he shall come into another world, he shall not be without a house, nor without a horse, nor without gold and silver; and the mare shall give him milk, and bring him forth more horses, till he be well stored in the other world; for they believe that, after their death, they shall be eating and drinking in that other world, and solacing themselves with their wives, as they did here.

And after the emperor is thus interred, no man shall be so hardy as to speak of him before his friends. Many cause themselves to be interred privately by night, in wild places, and the grass put again over the pit, to grow; or they cover the pit with gravel and sand, that no man shall perceive where the pit is, to the intent that never after may his friends have mind or remembrance of him. Then they say that he is ravished into another world, where he is a greater lord than he was here.

And then, after the death of the emperor, the seven lineages assemble together, and choose his eldest son, or the next after him of his blood; and thus they say to him: "We will, and we pray and ordain, that you be our lord and our emperor." And then he answers, "If you will that I reign over you as lord, each of you do as I shall command him, either to abide or go; and whomsoever I command to be slain, that anon he be slain." And they answer all, with one voice, "Whatsoever you command it shall be done." Then says the emperor, "Now understand well that my word from henceforth is sharp and biting as a sword." After, they set him upon a black steed, and so bring him to a chair full richly arrayed, and there they crown him. And then all the cities and good towns send him rich presents, so that at that day he shall have more than sixty chariots laden with gold and silver, besides jewels of gold and precious stones, that lords give him, that are beyond estimation; and also horses and cloths of gold, and camakas, and cloth of Tartary, that are innumerable.

CHAPTER XXIV.

OF THE REALM OF THARSE, AND THE LANDS AND KINGDOMS TOWARD THE NORTH PARTS, IN COMING DOWN FROM THE LAND OF CATHAY.

This land of Cathay is in Central Asia; and after, on this side, is Asia the Greater. The kingdom of Cathay borders toward the west on the kingdom of Tharse, of which was one of the kings that came with presents to our Lord in Bethlehem, and some of those who are of the lineage of that king are Christians. In Tharse they eat no flesh, and drink no wine. And on this side, toward the west, is the kingdom of Turkestan, which extends toward the west to the kingdom of Persia; and toward the north to the kingdom of Chorasm. In the center of Turkestan are but few good cities; but the best city of that land is called Octorar. There are great pastures, but little corn; and therefore, for the most part, they are all herdsmen; and they lie in tents, and drink a kind of ale made of honey.

And after it, on this side, is the kingdom of Chorasm (Khorasan), which is a good land and a plentiful, but without wine. It has a desert toward the east, which extends more than a hundred days' journey; and the best city of that country is called Chorasm, from which the country takes its name. The people of that country are hardy warriors. And on this side is the kingdom of Comania, whence were driven the Comanians that dwelt in Greece. This is one of the greatest kingdoms of the world, but it is not all inhabited; for in one part there is so great cold that no man may dwell there; and in another part there is so great heat that no man can endure it; and also there are so many flies, that no man may know on what side he may turn him. In that country is but little wood or trees bearing fruit, or others. They lie in tents; and they burn the dung of beasts for want of wood.

This kingdom descends on this side toward us, and toward Prussia and Russia. And through that country runs the River Ethille, which is one of the greatest rivers in the world; and it freezes so strongly all year that many times men have fought upon the ice with great armies, both parties on foot, having quitted their horses for the time; and what on horse and foot, more than 200,000 persons on every side. And between that river and the great Sea of Ocean, which they call the Maure Sea, lie all these kingdoms. And toward the head beneath in that realm is the mountain of Chotaz, which is the highest mountain in the world; and it is between the Maure Sea and the Caspian Sea. There is a very narrow and dangerous passage to go toward India; and therefore King Alexander made there a strong city, which they call Alexandria, to guard the country, that no man should pass without his leave; and now men call that city the Gate of Hell.

And the principal city of Comania is called Sarak, which is one of the three ways to go into India; but by this way no great multitude of people can pass unless it be in winter; and that passage men call the Derbent. The other way is from the city of Turkestan, by Persia; and by that way is many days' journey by desert; and the third way is from Comania, by the Great Sea, and by the kingdom of Abchaz.

And you shall understand that all these kingdom and lands above mentioned, unto Prussia and Russia, are all subject to the Great Chan of Cathay, and many other countries that border on them.

CHAPTER XXV.

OF THE EMPEROR OF PERSIA, AND OF THE LAND OF DARKNESS, AND OF OTHER KINGDOMS THAT BELONG TO THE GREAT CHAN OF CATHAY, AND OTHER LANDS OF HIS, UNTO THE SEA OF GREECE.

Now, since I have spoken of the lands and the kingdoms toward the north part, in coming down from the land of Cathay unto the lands of the Christians, toward Prussia and Russia, I will speak of other lands and kingdoms coming down toward the right side, unto the Sea of Greece, toward the land of the Christians. And since, after India and Cathay, the Emperor of Persia is the greatest lord, I will tell you of the kingdom of Persia.

He hath two kingdom; the first begins toward the east, toward the kingdom of Turkestan, and extends toward the west to the River Pison, which is one of the four rivers that come out of Paradise. And on another side it extends toward the north to the Caspian Sea, and toward the south to the desert of India. And this country is good, and pleasant, and full of people, and contains many good cities. But the two principal cities are Boycurra and Seornergant, that some men call Sormagant. The other kingdom of Persia extends toward the River Pison, and the parts of the west, to the kingdom of Media, and from the Great Armenia toward the north to the Caspian Sea, and toward the south to the land of India. That is also a good and rich land, and it hath three great principal cities, Messabor, Caphon, and Sarmassane.

And then after is Armenia, in which were formerly four kingdoms; it is a noble country, and full of goods. And it begins at Persia, and extends toward the west in length unto Turkey, and in breadth it extends to the city of Alexandria, that now is called the Gate of Hell, that I spoke of before, under the kingdom of Media. In this Armenia are many good cities, but Taurizo is most of name.

After this is the kingdom of Media, which is very long, but not broad, beginning, toward the east, with the land of Persia, and

India the Less; and it extends toward the west to the kingdom of Chaldea, and toward the north toward Little Armenia. In that kingdom of Media are many great hills and little of level ground. Saracens dwell there, and another kind of people called Cordines. The two best cities of that kingdom are Sarras and Karemen.

After that is the kingdom of Georgia, which commences toward the east, at the great mountain called Abzor, and contains many people of different nations. And men call the country Alamo. This kingdom extends toward Turkey, and toward the Great Sea; and toward the south it borders on the Greater Armenia. And there are two kingdoms in that country, the kingdom of Georgia and the kingdom of Abchaz; and always in that country are two kings, both Christians; but the King of Georgia is in subjection to the Great Chan. And the King of Abchaz has the stronger country, and he always vigorously defends his country against all who assail him, so that no man may reduce him to subjection.

In that kingdom of Abchaz is a great marvel; for a province of the country, that has well in circuit three days, which they call Hanyson, is all covered with darkness, without any brightness or light, so that no man can see there, nor no man dare enter into it. And, nevertheless, they of the country say that sometimes men hear voices of people, and horses neighing, and cocks crowing; and men know well that men dwell there, but they know not what men. And they say that the darkness befell by miracle of God; for a cursed emperor of Persia, named Saures, pursued all the Christians to destroy them, and to compel them to make sacrifice to his idols, and rode with a great host, in all that ever he might, to confound the Christians.

And then, in that country, dwelt many good Christians who left their goods, and would have fled into Greece; and when they were in a plain, called Megon, anon this cursed emperor met with them with his host, to have slain them and cut them to pieces. And the Christians kneeled to the ground, and made their prayers to God to succor them; and anon a great thick cloud came, and covered the emperor and all his host; and so they remain in that manner, that they may go out on no side; and so shall they ever more abide in darkness till doomsday, by the miracles of God. And then the Christians went where they liked at their own pleasure, without hinderance of any creature. And you shall understand that out of that land of darkness issues a great river, that shows well there are people dwelling there, by many ready tokens; but no man dare enter into it.

And know well that in the kingdoms of Georgia, Abchaz, and the Little Armenia, are good and devout Christian; for they shrive and housel themselves always once or twice in the week; and many housel themselves every day.

Also, after, on this side, is Turkey, which borders on the Great Armenia. And there are many provinces, as Cappadocia, Saure, Brique, Quesiton, Pytan, and Gemethe; and in each of these are many good cities. This Turkey extends to the city of Sathala, that sitteth upon the Sea of Greece, and so it borders on Syria. Syria is a great and a good country, as I have told you before. And also it has, toward Upper India, the kingdom of Chaldea, extending from the mountains of Chaldea toward the east to the city of Nineveh on the River Tigris; in breadth it begins toward the north, at the city of Maraga, and extends toward the south to the Sea of Ocean. Chaldea is a level country, with few hills and few rivers.

After this is the kingdom of Mesopotamia, which begins toward the east, at the River Tigris, at a city called Moselle, and extends toward the west to the River Euphrates, to a city called Roianz; and in length it extends from the mountain of Armenia to the desert of India the Less. This is a good and level country; but it has few rivers. There are but two mountains in that country, of which one is called Symar, the other Lyson. This land borders on the kingdom of Chaldea.

There are also, toward the south parts, many countries and regions, as the land of Ethiopia, which borders toward the east on the great deserts, toward the west on the kingdom of Nubia, toward the south on the kingdom of Mauritania, and toward the north on the Red Sea. After is Mauritania, which extends from the mountains of Ethiopia to Upper Lybia. And that country lies along from the Ocean Sea toward the south, and toward the north it borders on Nubia and Upper Lybia. The men of Nubia are Christians. And it extends trom the lands above mentioned to the deserts of Egypt, of which I have spoken before. And after is Upper and Lower Lybia, which descends low down, toward the great Sea of Spain, in which country are many kingdoms and different people.

CHAPTER XXVI.

OF THE COUNTRIES AND ISLANDS BEYOND THE LAND OF CATHAY, AND OF THE FRUITS THERE; AND OF TWENTY-TWO KINGS IN-CLOSED WITHIN THE MOUNTAINS.

IN passing by the land of Cathay toward Upper India and toward Bucharia, men pass by a kingdom called Caldilhe, which is a very fair country. And there grows a kind of fruit like gourds, which, when they are ripe, men cut in two, and find within a little beast, in flesh, bone, and blood, as though it were a little lamb, without wool. And men eat both the fruit and the beast, and that is a great marvel. Of that fruit I have eaten; and I told them of as great a marvel to them that is amongst us, and that was of the barnacles. For I told them that in our country were trees that bear a fruit that becomes flying birds; and those that fall in the water live; and those that fall on the earth die anon; and they are right good for man's meat. And thereof had they also great marvel, that some of them thought it was an impossibility.

In that country are long apples, of good flavor, whereof there are more than a hundred in a cluster; and they have great long leaves and large, of two feet long or more. And in that country, and in other countries thereabout, grow many trees that bear clove-gylofres and nutmegs, and great nuts of India, and of canelle, and many other spices. And there are vines which bear grapes so large that a strong man would have enough to do to carry one cluster. In that same region are the mountains of Caspia, which are called Uber in the country. Between those mountains are inclosed the Jews of ten lineages, who are called Gog and Magog; and they may not go out on any side.

There were inclosed twenty-two kings with their people, that dwelt between the mountains of Scythia. King Alexander drove them between those mountains, and there he thought to inclose them through work of his men. But when he saw that he might not do it, nor bring it to an end, he prayed to the God of Nature that He would perform that which he had begun. And although he was a pagan, and not worthy to be heard, yet God of His grace closed the mountains together, so that they dwell there fast locked and inclosed with high mountains all about, except only on one side, and on that side is the Caspian Sea. Men say they shall come out in the time of Antichrist, and that they shall make great slaughter of the Christians, and therefore all the Jews that dwell in all lands learn always to speak Hebrew, in hope that when the other Jews shall go out, they may understand their speech, and so lead them into Christendom, to destroy the Christians. For the Jews say that they know well, by their prophecies, that they of Caspia shall go out, and spread through all the world, and that the Christians shall be under subjection as long as they have been in subjection to them.

And if you will know how they shall find their way, after what I have heard say I will tell you. In the time of Antichrist, a fox shall make there his trail, and burrow a hole where King Aléxander made the gates; and so long he shall burrow and pierce the earth, till he shall pass through, toward that people. And when they see the fox they shall have great wonder of him, because they never saw such a beast; for of all other beasts they have some inclosed among them, except the fox. And then they shall hunt him, and pursue him so close, till he arrive at the same place he came from; and then they shall dig and burrow so strongly, till they find the gates that king Alexander made of immense stones, well cemented and made strong for the mastery; and those gates they shall break, and so go out, by finding that issue.

From that land men go toward the land of Bucharia, where are very evil and cruel people. In that land are trees that bear wool, as though it were of sheep, whereof men make clothes, and all things that may be made of wool. In that country are many ipotaynes, that dwell sometimes in the water and sometimes on the land; and they are half man and half horse, as I have said before; and they eat men, when they may take them. And there are rivers of water that are very bitter, three times more than is the water of the sea. In that country are many griffins, more abundant than in any other country. Some men say that they have the body upward of an eagle, and beneath of a lion; and that is true. But one griffin has a greater body and is stronger than eight lions, and greater and stronger than a hundred eagles. For one griffin there will carry, flying to his nest, a great horse, or two oxen yoked together, as they go at the plow. For he has his talons so long, and so large and great, as though they were horns of great oxen, or of bulls, or of kine, so that men make cups of them to drink out of; and of their ribs, and of the feathers of their win s, men make bows full strong, to shoot with arrows and darts. From thence men go, by many days, through the land of Prester John, the great Emperor of India. And they call his kingdom the Isle of Pentexoire.

CHAPTER XXVII.

OF THE ROYAL ESTATE OF PRESTER JOHN; AND OF A RICH MAN THAT MADE A MARVELOUS CASTLE, AND CALLED IT PARADISE, AND OF HIS CUNNING.

THIS emperor, Prester John, possesses very extensive territory, and has many very noble cities and good towns in his realm, and many great and large isles. For all the country of India is divided into isles, by the great floods that come from Paradise, that separate all the land into many parts. And also in the sea he has full many isles. And the best city in the Isle of Pentexoire is Nyse, a very royal city, noble and very rich. This Prester John has under him many kings, and many isles and many divers people of divers conditions. And this land is full good and rich, but not so rich as the land of the Great Chan. For the merchants come not thither so commonly to buy merchandise, as they do in the land of the Great Chan, for it is too far.

And on the other side, in the Isle of Cathay, men find all things needful to man, cloths of gold, of silk, and spicery. And therefore, although men have them cheap in the Isle of Prester John, they dread the long way and the great perils in the sea. For in many places of the sea are great rocks of stone of adamant (loadstone), which of its nature draws iron to it; and therefore there pass no ships that have either bonds or nails of iron in them; and if they do, anon the rocks of adamant draw them to them, that they may never go thence. I myself have seen afar in that sea, as though it had been a great isle full of trees and bushes, full of thorns and briers, in great plenty; and the shipmen told us that all that was of ships that were drawn thither by the adamants, for the iron that was in them. And of the rottenness and other things that were within the ships, grew such bushes, and thorns, and briers, and green grass, and such kinds of things; and of the masts and the sail-yards, it seemed a great wood or a grove.

And such rocks are in many places thereabout. And therefore merchants dare not pass there, except they know well the passages, or unless they have good pilots. And also they dread the long way, and, therefore, they go to Cathay, because it is nearer; and yet it is not so nigh but men must travel by sea and land eleven or twelve months, from Genoa or from Venice, to Cathay. And yet is the land of Prester John more far, by many dreadful days' journey. And the merchants pass by the kingdom of Persia, and go to a city called Hermes, because Hermes the philosopher founded it. And after that they pass an arm of the sea, and then they go to another city called Golbache; and there they find merchandise, and as great abundance of parrots as men find here of geese. In that country is but little wheat or barley, and therefore they eat rice and honey, milk, cheese, and fruit.

This emperor, Prester John, takes always to wife the daughter of the Great Chan; and the Great Chan also in the same wise the daughter of Prester John. For they two are the greatest lords under the firmament.

In the land of Prester John are many divers things and many precious stones, so great and so large, that men make of them plates, dishes, cups, etc. And many other marvels are there, that it were too long to put in a book. But I will tell you of his principal isles, and of his estate, and of his law. This Emperor Prester John is a Christian, and a great part of his country also; but they have not all the articles of our faith. They believe in the Father, Son, and Holy Ghost, and they are very devout and true to one another. And he has under him seventy-two provinces, and in every province is a king, all which kings are tributary to Prester John. And in his lordships are many great marvels, for in his country is the sea called the Gravelly Sea, which is all gravel and sand, without a drop of water; and it ebbs and flows in great waves, as other seas do, and it is never still. And no man can pass that sea with ships, and, therefore, no man knows what land is beyond that sea. And although it has no water, men find therein, and on the banks, very good fish, of different nature and shape from what are found in any other sea; and they are of very good taste, and delicious to eat.

Three days from that sea are great mountains, out of which runs a great river which comes from Paradise, and it is full of precious stones, without a drop of water, and it runs through the desert, on one side, so that it makes the Gravelly Sea where it ends. And that river runs only three days in the week, and brings with it great stones and the rocks also therewith, and that in great plenty. And when they are entered into the Gravelly Sea they are seen no more. And in those three days that that river runneth, no man dare enter into it, but in the other days men dare enter well enough. Beyond that river, more up toward the deserts, is a great plain all gravelly between the mountains; and in that plain, every day at sunrise, small trees begin to grow, and they grow till midday, bearing fruit; but no man dare take of that fruit, for it is a thing of fairie. And after midday they decrease and enter again into the earth, so that at sunset they appear no more; and so they do every day.

In that desert are many wild men, hideous to look on, and horned; and they speak naught, but grunt like pigs. And there is also great plenty of wild dogs. And there are many parrots, which speak of their own nature, and salute men that go through the deserts, and speak to them as plainly as though it were a man. And they that speak well have a large tongue, and have five toes upon each foot. And there are also others which have but three toes upon each foot, and they speak but little.

This Emperor Prester John, when he goes to battle against any other lord, has no banners borne before him; but he has three large crosses of gold full of precious stones; and each cross is set in a chariot full richly arrayed. And to keep each cross are appointed ten thousand men of arms, and more than one hundred thousand footmen. And this number of people is independent of the chief army. And when he has no war, but rides with a private company, he has before him but one plain cross of wood, in remembrance that Jesus Christ suffered death upon a wooden cross. And they carry before him also a platter of gold full of earth, in token that his nobleness, and his might, and his flesh, shall turn to earth. And he has borne before him also a vessel of silver, full of noble jewels of gold and precious stones, in token of his lordship, nobility, and power. He dwells commonly in the city of Susa, and there is his principal palace, which is so rich and noble that no man can conceive it without seeing it.

And above the chief tower of the palace are two round pommels of gold, in each of which are two large carbuncles, which shine bright in the night. And the principal gates of his palace are of the precious stones called sardonyx; and the border and bars are of ivory; and the windows of the halls and chambers are of crystal; and the tables, on which men eat, some are of emeralds, some of amethyst, and some of gold, full of precious stones; and the pillars that support the tables are of the same precious stones. Of the steps approaching his throne, where he sits at meat, one is of onyx, another crystal, another green jasper, another amethyst, another sardonyx, another carnelian, and the seventh, on which he sets his feet, is of chrysolite. All these steps are bordered with fine gold, with the other precious stones, set with great orient pearls. The sides of the seat of his throne are of emeralds, and bordered full nobly with gold, and dubbed with other precious stones and great pearls. All the pillars in his chamber are of fine gold with precious stones, and with many carbuncles, which give great light by night to all people. And although the carbuncle gives light enough, nevertheless at all times a vessel of crystal, full of balm, is burning, to give good smell and odor to the emperor, and to expel all wicked airs and corruptions.

The frame of his bed is of fine sapphires blended with gold, to make him sleep well. He hath also a very fair and noble palace in the city of Nice, where he dwells when he likes; but the air is not so temperate as it is at the city of Susa. And you shall understand that in his country, and in the countries surrounding, men eat but once in the day, as they do in the court of the Great Chan. And more than thirty thousand persons eat every day in his court, besides goers and comers, but these thirty thousand persons spend not so much as twelve thousand of our country.

This Emperor Prester John has evermore seven kings with him, to serve him, who share their service by certain months; and with these kings serve always seventy-two dukes and three hundred and sixty earls. And all the days of the year, twelve archbishops and twenty bishops eat in his household and in his court. And the Patriarch of St. Thomas is there what the Pope is here. And the archbishops, and the bishops, and the abbots in that country, are all kings. And each of these great lords knows well the attendance of his service. One is master of his household, another is his chamberlain, another serveth him with a dish, another with a cup, another is steward, another is marshal, another is prince of his arms; and thus is he full nobly and royally served. And his land extends in extreme breadth four months' journey, and in length out of measure, including all the isles under earth, that we suppose to be under us.

Near the Isle of Pentexoire, which is the land of Prester John, is a great isle, long and broad, called Milsterak, which is in the lordship of Prester John. That isle is very rich. There was dwelling not long since a rich man, named Gatholonabes, who was full of tricks and subtle deceits. He had a fair and strong castle in a mountain, so strong and noble that no man could devise a fairer or a stronger. And he had caused the mountain to be all walled about with a strong and fair wall, within which walls he had the fairest garden that might be imagined; and therein were trees bearing all manner of fruits, all kinds of herbs of virtue and of good smell, and all other herbs also that bear fair flowers. And he had also in that garden many fair wells, and by them he had made fair halls and fair chambers, painted all with gold and azure, representing many divers things and many divers stories.

There were also beasts and birds which sung full delectably, and moved by craft, that it seemed that they were alive. And he had also in his garden all kinds of birds and beasts, that men might have play or sport to behold them. And he had also in that place the fairest damsels that might be found under the age of fifteen years, and the fairest young striplings that men might get of that same age; and they were all clothed full richly in clothes of gold; and he said they were angels. And he had also caused to be made three fair and noble wells, all surrounded with stone of jasper and crystal, diapered with gold, and set with precious stones and great orient pearls. And he had made a conduit under the earth, so that the three wells, at his will, should run one with milk, another with wine, and another with honey. And that place he called Paradise. And when any good knight, who was hardy and noble, came to see this royalty, he would lead him into Paradise, and show him these wonderful things, for his sport, and the marvelous and delicious song of divers birds, and the fair damsels, and the fair wells of milk, wine, and honey, running plentifully.

There he would let divers instruments of music sound in a high tower, so merrily that it was joy to hear, and no man should see the craft thereof; and those he said were angels of God, and that place was Paradise, that God had promised to His friends, saying, "I will give you a land flowing with milk and honey." And then he would make them drink of certain drink, whereof anon they should be drunk; after which they seemed to have greater delight than they had before. And then would he say to them, that if they would die for him and for his love, after their death they should come to his Paradise; and they should be of the age of the damsels, and they should play with them. And after that he would put them in a fairer Paradise, where they should see the God of Nature visibly, in His majesty and bliss. And then would he show them his intent, and tell them, if they would go and slay such a lord or such a man who was his enemy, or disobedient to his will, they should not fear to do it, or to be slain themselves in doing it; for after their death he would put them into another Paradise that was a hundred-fold fairer than any of the others; and there should they dwell with the fairest damsels that might be, and play with them evermore.

And thus went many divers lusty bachelors to slay great lords in divers countries, that were his enemies, in hopes to have that Paradise. And thus he was often revenged of his enemies by his subtle deceits and false tricks. But when the worthy men of the country had perceived this subtle falsehood of this Gatholonabes, they assembled with force, and assailed his castle, and slew him, and destroyed all the fair places of that Paradise. The place of the wells and of the walls and of many other things are yet clearly to be seen, but the riches are clean gone. And it is not long ago since that place was destroyed.

CHAPTER XXVIII.

OF THE DEVIL'S HEAD IN THE PERILOUS VALLEY; AND OF THE CUSTOMS OF PEOPLE IN DIVERS ISLES THAT ARE ABOUT, IN THE LORDSHIP OF PRESTER JOHN.

NEAR that isle of Mistorak, upon the left side, nigh to the river of Pison, is a marvelous thing. There is a vale between the mountains which extends nearly four miles; and some call it the Enchanted Vale, some call it the Vale of Devils, and some the Perilous Vale. In that vale men hear oftentimes great tempests and thunders, and great murmurs and noises, day and night; and great noise, as it were, of tabors, and nakeres, and trumpets, as though it were of a great feast. This vale is all full of devils, and has been always; and men say there that it is one of the entrances of hell. In that vale is great plenty of gold and silver; wherefore many misbelieving men, and many Christians also, oftentimes go in, to have of the treasure; but few return, especially of the misbelieving men, for they are anon strangled by the devils.

And in the center of that vale, under a rock, is a head and the visage of a devil bodily, full horrible and dreadful to see, and it shows but the head to the shoulders. But there is no man in the world so bold, Christian or other, but he would be in dread to behold it, and he would feel almost dead with fear, so hideous is it to behold. For he looks at every man so sharply with dreadful eyes, that are ever moving and sparkling like fire, and changes and stirs so often in divers manners, with so horrible a countenance, that no man dare approach toward him. And from him issue smoke, and stink, and fire, and so much abomination that scarce any man may endure there. But the good Christians, that are stable in their faith, enter without peril; for they will first shrive them, and mark them with the sign of the holy cross, so that the fiends have no power over them. But although they are without peril, yet they are not without dread when they see the devils visibly and bodily all about them, that make full many divers assaults and menaces, in air and on earth, and terrify them with strokes of thunder-blasts and of tempests. And the greatest fear is that God will take vengeance then of that which men have misdone against His will.

And you shall understand that when my fellows and I were in this vale, we were in great thought whether we durst put our bodies in aventure, to go in or not, in the protection of God; and some of our fellows agreed to enter, and some not. So there were with us two worthy men, friars minors of Lombardy, who said that if any man would enter they would go in with us; and when they had said so, upon the gracious trust of God and of them, we heard Mass, and every man was shriven and houseled; and then we entered, fourteen persons, but at our going out we were but nine. And so we never knew whether our fellows were lost, or had turned back for fear; but we never saw them after. They were two men of Greece, and three of Spain. And our other fellows, that would not go in with us, went by another road to be before us; and so they were.

And thus we passed that Perilous Vale, and found therein gold and silver, and precious stones, and rich jewels, in great plenty, both here and there, as it seemed; but whether it was as it seemed I know not, for I touched none; because the devils are so subtle to make a thing seem otherwise than it is, to deceive mankind; and therefore I touched none; and also because that I would not be put out of my devotion, for I was more devout then than ever I was before or after, and all for the dread of fiends that I saw in divers figures; and also for the great multitude of dead bodies that I saw there lying by the way, in all the vale, as though there had been a battle between two kings, and the mightiest of the country, and that the greater party had been discomfited and slain. And I believe that hardly should any country have so many people in it as lay slain in that vale, as it seemed to us, which was a hideous sight to see. And I marveled much that there were so many, and the bodies all whole, without rotting; but I believe that fiends made them seem to be so fresh, without rotting. And many of them were in habits of Christian men; but I believe they were such as went in for covetousness of the treasure that was there, and had overmuch feebleness in faith; so that their hearts might not endure in the belief for dread. And therefore we were the more devout a great deal; and yet we were cast down and beaten down many times to the hard

earth by winds, and thunders, and tempests; but evermore God of
His grace helped us. And so we passed that Perilous Vale without
peril and without incumbrance, thanked be Almighty God!

After this, beyond the vale, is a great isle, the inhabitants of which
are great giants of twenty-eight or thirty feet long, with no clothing
but skins of beasts, that they hang upon them; and they eat nothing
but raw flesh, and drink milk of beasts. They have no houses to lie
in. And they eat more gladly man's flesh than any other flesh. Into
that isle dare no man enter, and if they see a ship, and men therein,
anon they enter into the sea to take them. And men told us that in
an isle beyond that were giants of greater stature, some of forty-five
or fifty feet long, and even, as some men say, of fifty cubits long;
but I saw none of those; for I had no lust to go to those parts, because that no man comes either into that isle or into the other but
he will be devoured anon. And among those giants are sheep as
great as oxen here, which bear great rough wool. Of the sheep I
have seen many times. And men have said many times those
giants take men, in the sea, out of their ships, and bring them to
land, two in one hand and two in the other, eating them going, all
raw and alive.

In another isle, toward the north, in the Sea of Ocean, are very
evil women, who have precious stones in their eyes; and if they behold any man with wrath, they slay him with the look.

After that is another isle, where women make great sorrow when
their children are born, and when they die, they make great feasts,
and great joy and revel, and then they cast them into a great burning fire. And those that love well their husbands, if their husbands
die, they cast themselves also into the fire, with their children, and
burn them. In that isle they make their king always by election;
and they choose him not for nobleness or riches, but such a one as
is of good manners and condition, and therewithal just; and also
that he be of great age, and that he have no children.

In that isle men are very just, and they do just judgments in
every cause, both of rich and poor, small and great, according to
their trespasses. And the king may not judge a man to death
without assent of his barons and other wise men of council, and
unless all the court agree thereto. And if the king himself do any
homicide or crime, as to slay a man, or any such case, he shall die
for it; but he shall not be slain as another man; but they forbid, on
pain of death, that any man be so bold as to make him company or
to speak with him, or give or sell him meat or drink; and so shall

he die disgracefully. They spare no man that has trespassed, either for love, or favor, or riches, or nobility; but that he shall have according to what he has done.

Beyond that isle is another, where is a great multitude of people, who will not eat flesh of hares, hens, or geese; and yet they breed them in abundance, to see and behold them only; but they eat flesh of all other beasts, and drink milk. In that country they take their daughters and their sisters to wife, and their other kinswomen. And if there be ten or twelve men, or more, dwelling in a house, the wife of each of them shall be common to them all that dwell in that house; so that every man may lie with whom he will of them on one night, and with another, another night. And if she have any child she may give it to what man she list that has kept company with her; so that no man knows there whether the child be his or another's. And if any man say to them that they nourish other men's children, they answer that so do other men theirs.

In that country, and in all India, are great plenty of cockodrills, a sort of long serpent, as I have said before; and in the night they dwell in the water, and in the day upon the land, in rocks and cavers; and they eat no meat in winter, but lie as in a dream, as do serpents. These serpents slay men, and they eat them weeping; and when they eat they move the upper jaw, and not the lower jaw; and they have no tongue. In that country, and in many others beyond, and also in many on this side, men sow the seed of cotton; and they sow it every year, and then it grows to small trees, which bear cotton. And so do men every year, so that there is plenty of cotton at all times.

In this isle also, and in many others, there is a manner of wood, hard and strong; and whoever covers the coals of that wood under the ashes thereof, the coals will remain alive a year or more. And among other trees there are nut-trees, that bear nuts as great as a man's head. There are also animals called orafles, which are called, in Arabia, gerfauntz. They are spotted, and a little higher than a horse, with a neck twenty cubits long; and the croup and tail are like those of a hart; and one of them may look over a high house. And there are also in that country many chameleons; and there are very great serpents, some one hundred and twenty feet long, of divers colors, as rayed, red, green and yellow, blue and black, and all speckled. And there are others that have crests upon their heads; and they go upon their feet upright. And there are also wild swine of many colors, as great as oxen in our country, all spotted like young fawns. And there are also hedgehogs, as great as wild swine, which we call porcupines. And there are many other extraordinary animals.

CHAPTER XXIX.

OF THE GOODNESS OF THE PEOPLE OF THE ISLE OF BRAGMAN— OF KING ALEXANDER, AND WHY THE EMPEROR OF INDIA IS CALLED PRESTER JOHN.

And beyond that isle is another isle, great and rich, where are good and true people, and of good living after their belief, and of good faith, and although they are not christened, yet by natural law they are full of all virtue, and eschew all vices; for they are not proud, nor covetous, nor envious, nor wrathful, nor gluttonous, nor lecherous; nor do they to any man otherwise than they would that other men did to them; and in this point they fulfill the ten commandments of God. And they care not for possessions or riches; and they lie not, nor do they swear, but say simply yea and nay; for they say he that sweareth will deceive his neighbor; and therefore all that they do they do it without oath. And that isle is called the Isle of Bragman, and some men call it the Land of Faith; and through it runs a great river called Thebe.

And in general all the men of those isles, and of all the borders thereabout, are truer than in any other country thereabout, and more just than others in all things. In that isle is no thief, no murderer, no common woman, no poor beggar, and no man was ever slain in that country. And they be as chaste, and lead as good a life, as though they were monks; and they fast all days. And because they are so true, and so just, and so full of all good conditions, they are never grieved with tempests, nor with thunder and lightning, nor with hail, nor with pestilence, nor with war, nor with famine, nor with any other tribulation, as we are many times amongst us for our sins; wherefore it appears evident that God loveth them for their good deeds. They believe well in God that made all things, and worship Him; and they prize no earthly riches; and they live full orderly, and so soberly in meat and drink, that they live right long. And the most part of them die without sickness, when nature faileth them for old age.

And it befell, in King Alexander's time, that he purposed to conquer that isle; but when they of the country heard it, they sent messengers to him with letters, that said thus: "What may we be now to that man to whom all the world is insufficient? Thou shalt find nothing in us to cause thee to war against us; for we have no riches, nor do we desire any; and all the goods of our country are in common. Our meat, with which we sustain our bodies, is our riches; and instead of treasure of gold and silver, we make our treasure of acorns and pease, and to love one another. And to apparel our bodies we use a simple cloth to wrap our carcass. Our wives are not arrayed to make any man pleased. When men labor to array the body, to make it seem fairer than God made it, they do great sin; for man should not devise nor ask greater beauty than God hath ordained him to have at his birth. The earth ministereth to us two things: our livelihood, that cometh of the earth that we live by, and our sepulcher after our death. We have been in perpetual peace till now that thou art come to disinherit us; and also we have a king, not to do justice to every man, for he shall find no forfeit among us; but to keep nobleness, and to show that we are obedient, we have a king. For justice has among us no place; for we do to no man otherwise than we desire that men do to us, so that righteousness or vengeance has naught to do among us; so that thou mayest take nothing from us but our good peace, that always hath endured among us." And when King Alexander had read these letters he thought that he should do great sin to trouble them.

There is another isle called Oxidrate, and another called Gymnosophe, where there are also good people, and full of good faith; and they hold, for the most part, the same good conditions and customs, and good manners, as men of the country above mentioned; but they all go naked. Into that isle entered King Alexander, to see the customs; and when he saw their great faith, and the truth that was amongst them, he said that he would not grieve them, and bade them ask of him what they would have of him, riches or anything else, and they should have it with good-will. And they answered that he was rich enough that had meat and drink to sustain the body with; for the riches of this world, that is transitory, are of no worth; but if it were in his power to make them immortal, thereof would they pray him, and thank him.

And Alexander answered them that it was not in his power to do it, because he was mortal, as they were. And then they asked him why he was so proud, and so fierce, and so busy, to put all the world under his subjection, "Right as thou wert a God, and hast no term of this life, neither day nor hour; and covetest to have all the world at thy command, that shall leave thee without fail, or thou leave it. And right as it hath been to other men before thee, right so it shall be to others after thee, and from hence shalt thou carry nothing; but as thou wert born naked, right so all naked shall thy body be turned into earth, that thou wert made of. Wherefore thou shouldest think, and impress it on thy mind, that nothing is immortal but only God, that made all things." By which answer Alexander was greatly astonished and abashed, and all confused departed from them.

Many other isles there are in the land of Prester John, and many great marvels, that were too long to tell, both of his riches and of his nobleness, and of the great plenty also of precious stones that he has. I think that you know well now, and have heard say, why this emperor is called Prester John. There was some time an emperor there, who was a worthy and a full noble prince, that had Christian knights in his company, as he has that now is. So it befell that he had great desire to see the service in the church among Christians; and then Christendom extended beyond the sea, including all Turkey, Syria, Tartary, Jerusalem, Palestine, Arabia, Aleppo, and all the land of Egypt. So it befell that this emperor came, with a Christian knight with him, into a church in Egypt; and it was the Saturday in Whitsuntide. And the bishop was conferring orders; and he beheld and listened to the service full attentively; and he asked the Christian knight what men of degree they should be that the prelate had before him; and the knight answered and said that they were priests. And then the emperor said that he would no longer be called king nor emperor, but priest; and that he would have the name of the first priest that went out of the Church; and his name was John. And so, evermore since, he is called Prester John.

CHAPTER XXX.

OF THE HILLS OF GOLD THAT ANTS KEEP; AND OF THE FOUR STREAMS THAT COME FROM TERRESTRIAL PARADISE.

TOWARD the east of Prester John's land is a good and great isle called Taprobane, and it is very fruitful; and the king thereof is rich, and is under the obeisance of Prester John. And there they always make their king by election. In that isle are two summers and two winters; and men harvest the corn twice a year; and in all seasons of the year the gardens are in flower. There dwell good people, and reasonable; and many Christian men among them, who are so rich that they know not what to do with their goods. Of old time, when men passed from the land of Prester John unto that isle, men made ordinance to pass by ship in twenty three days or more; but now men pass by ship in seven days. And men may see the bottom of the sea in many places; for it is not very deep.

Beside that isle, toward the east, are two other isles, one called Orille, the other Argyte, of which all the land is mines of gold and silver. And those isles are just where the Red Sea separates from the Ocean Sea. And in those isles men see no stars so clearly as in other places; for there appears only one clear star called Canopus. And there the moon is not seen in all the lunation, except in the second quarter. In the isle, also, of this Taprobane are great hills of gold, that ants keep full diligently.

And beyond the land, and isles, and deserts of Prester John's lordship, in going straight toward the east, men find nothing but mountains and great rocks; and there is the dark region, where no man may see, neither by day nor night, as they of the country say. And that desert, and that place of darkness, lasts from this coast unto Terrestrial Paradise, where Adam, our first father, and Eve were put, who dwelt there but a little while; and that is toward the east, at the beginning of the earth. But this is not that east that we call our east, on this half, where the sun rises to us; for when the sun is east in those parts toward Terrestrial Paradise, it is then midnight in our parts on this half, on account of the roundness of the earth, of which I have told you before; for our Lord God made the earth all round, in the middle of the firmament. And there have mountains and hills been, and valleys, which arose only from Noah's flood, that wasted the soft and tender ground, and fell down into valleys; and the hard earth and the rock remain mountains, when the soft and tender earth was worn away by the water, and fell, and became valleys.

Of Paradise I can not speak properly, for I was not there. It is far beyond; and I repent not going there, but I was not worthy. But as I have heard say of wise men beyond, I shall tell you with good will. Terrestrial Paradise, as wise men say, is the highest place of the earth; and it is so high that it nearly touches the circle of the moon there, as the moon makes her turn. For it is so high that the flood of Noah might not come to it, that would have covered all the earth of the world all about, and above and beneath, except Paradise. And this Paradise is inclosed all about with a wall, and men know not whereof it is; for the wall is covered all over with moss, as it seems; and it seems not that the wall is natural stone.

And that wall stretches from the south to the north; and it has but one entry, which is closed with burning fire, so that no man that is mortal dare enter.

And in the highest place of Paradise, exactly in the middle, is a well that casts out the four streams, which run by divers lands, of which the first is called Pison, or Ganges, that runs throughout India, or Emlak, in which river are many precious stones, and much lignum aloes, and much sand of gold. And the other river is called Nile, or Gyson, which goes through Ethiopia, and after through Egypt. And the other is called Tigris, which runs by Assyria, and by Armenia the Great. And the other is called Euphrates, which runs through Media, Armenia, and Persia. And men there beyond say that all the sweet waters of the world, above and beneath, take their beginning from the well of Paradise; and out of that well all waters come and go. The first river is called Pison, that is, in our language, Assembly: for many other rivers meet there, and go into that river. And some call it Ganges, from an Indian king, called Gangeres, because it ran through his land. And its water is in some places clear, and in some places troubled; in some places hot, and in some places cold. The second river is called Nile, or Gyson, for it is always troubled; and Gyson, in the language of Ethiopia, is to say Trouble, and in the language of Egypt also. The third river, called Tigris, is as much as to say, Fast Running; for it runs faster than any of the others. The fourth river is called Euphrates, that is to say, Well Bearing; for there grow upon that river corn, fruit, and other goods, in great plenty.

And you shall understand that no man that is mortal may approach to that Paradise; for by land no man may go for wild beasts, that are in the deserts, and for the high mountains, and great huge rocks, that no man may pass by for the dark places that are there; and by the rivers may no man go, for the water runs so roughly and so sharply, because it comes down so outrageously from the high places above, that it runs in so great waves that no ship may row or sail against it; and the water roars so, and makes so huge a noise, and so great a tempest, that no man may hear another in the ship, though he cried with all the might he could. Many great lords have essayed with great will, many times, to pass by those rivers toward Paradise, with full great companies; but they might not speed in their voyage; and many died for weariness of rowing against the strong waves; and many of them became blind, and many deaf, for the noise of the water; and some perished and were lost in the waves; so that no mortal man may approach to that place without special grace of God; so that of that place I can tell you no more.

CHAPTER XXXI.
OF THE CUSTOMS OF KINGS AND OTHERS THAT DWELL IN THE ISLES BORDERING ON PRESTER JOHN'S LAND.

FROM those isles that I have spoken of before, in the land of Prester John, that are under earth as to us, and of other isles that are further beyond, whoever will pursue them may come again right to the parts that he came from, and so environ all the earth; but what for the isles, what for the sea, and what for strong rowing, few people essay to pass that passage. And therefore men return from the isles beforesaid by other isles, coasting from the land of Prester John. And then come men, in returning, to an isle called Casson, which is full sixty days in length, and more than fifty in breadth. This is the best isle, and the best kingdom, that is in all those parts, except Cathay; and if the merchants used that country as much as they do Cathay it would be better than Cathay in a short time.

This country is well inhabited, and so full of cities and good towns, and inhabited with people, that when a man goes out of one city he sees another city before him. In that isle is great plenty of all goods to live with, and of all manner of spices; and there are great forests of chestnuts. The king of that isle is very rich and mighty; and yet he holds his land of the Great Chan, and is subject to him; for it is one of the twelve provinces which the Great Chan has under him, besides his own land, and other less isles, of which he has many.

From that kingdom come men, in returning, to another isle, called Rybothe, which also is under the Great Chan. It is a full good country, and rich in all goods, and wine and fruit, and all other riches. And the people of that country have no houses: but they dwell and lie all under tents made of black fern. And the principal city, and the most royal, is all walled with black and white stone; and all the streets, also, are paved with the same stones. In that city is no man so hardy as to shed blood of any man, nor of any beast, for the reverence of an idol that is worshiped there. And in that isle dwells the pope of their law, whom they call lobassy. This lobassy gives all the benefices, and other dignities, and all other things that belong to the idol.

In that isle they have a custom, in all the country, that when any man's father is dead, and the son wishes to do great honor to his father, he sends to all his friends, and to all his kin, and for religious men and priests, and for minstrels also, in great plenty; and then they bear the dead body unto a great hill, with great joy and solemnity; and when they have brought it thither, the chief prelate smites off the head, and lays it upon a great platter of gold and silver, if he be a rich man; and then he gives the head to the son; and then the son and his other kin sing and say many prayers; and then the priests, and the religious men, smite all the body of the dead man in pieces; and then they say certain prayers. And the birds of prey of all the country about know the custom for a long time before, and come flying above in the air, as eagles, kites, ravens, and other birds that eat flesh. And then the priests cast the bits of flesh, and each fowl takes what he may, and goes a little thence and eats it; and they do so whilst any piece of the dead body remains. And after that the preists sing with high voice, in their language, "Behold how worthy a man, and how good a man this was, that the angels of God came to seek him, and to bring him into Paradise." And then it seems to the son that he is highly worshiped when many birds, and fowls, and ravens come and eat his father; and he that has most number of fowls is most worshiped.

Then the son brings home with him all his kin, and his friends, and all the others to his house, and makes a great feast; and then all his friends make their boast how the fowls came thither, here five, here six, here ten, and there twenty, and so forth, and they rejoice greatly to speak thereof. And when they are at meat the son brings forth the head of his father, and thereof he serves of the flesh to his most special friends, as a dainty. And of the skull he makes a cup, and drinks out of it with his other friends in great devotion, in remembrance of the holy man that the angels of God had eaten. And that cup the son shall keep to drink out of all his life-time, in remembrance of his father.

From that land, in returning by ten days through the land of the Great Chan, is another good isle, and a great kingdom, where the king is full rich and mighty. And amongst the rich men of his country is a passing rich man, that is neither prince nor duke nor earl; but he has more that hold of him lands and other lordships; for he has every year, of annual rent, more than three hundred thousand horses charged with corn of divers grains and rice; and so he leads a full noble and delicate life, after the custom of the country; for he has every day fifty fair damsels, all maidens, that serve him evermore at his meat. And when he is at the table, they bring him his meat at every time, five and five together; and in bringing their service they sing a song.

And after that they cut his meat, and put it in his mouth; for he touches nothing, nor handles naught, but holds evermore his hands before him upon the table; for he has such long nails that he may take nothing, nor handle anything. For the nobleness of that country is to have long nails, and to make them grow always to be as long as men may; and there are many in that country that have their nails so long that they environ all the hand; and that is a great nobleness. And the nobleness of the women is to have small feet; and therefore, as soon as they are born, they bind their feet so tight that they may not grow half as nature would. And always these damsels, that I spoke of before, sing all the time that this rich man eateth; and when he eateth no more of his first course, then other five and five of fair damsels bring him his second course, always singing, as they did before; and so they do continually every day, to the end of his meat.

And in this manner he leads his life; and so they did before him that were his ancestors; and so shall they that come after him, without doing of any deeds of arms, but live evermore thus in ease, as a swine that is fed in a sty to be made fat. He has a full fair and rich palace, the walls of which are two miles in circuit; and he has within many fair gardens, and many fair halls and chambers; and the pavements of his halls and chambers are of gold and silver. And in the middle of one of his gardens is a little mountain, where there is a little meadow; and in that meadow is a little house, with towers and pinnacles, all of gold; and in that little house will he sit often to take the air and sport himself.

And you shall understand that of all these countries and isles, and of all the divers people that I have spoken of before, and of divers laws, and of divers beliefs that they have, there is none of them all but they have some reason and understanding in them, and that they have certain articles of our faith, and some good points of our belief; and they believe in God that created all things and made the world; but yet they can not speak perfectly (for there is no man to teach them), but only what they can devise by their natural understanding; for they have no knowledge of the Son nor of the Holy Ghost; but they can all speak of the Bible, namely of Genesis, of the Prophet's laws, and of the books of Moses.

And they say well that the creatures that they worship are no gods; but they worship them for the virtue that is in them. And of simulacres, and of idols, they say that there are no people but that they have simulacres; and they say that we Christian men have images, as of our Lady, and of other saints, that we worship; not the images of wood or of stone, but the saints in whose name they are made; for right as the books of the Scripture teach the clerks how and in what manner they shall believe, right so the images and the paintings teach the ignorant people to worship the saints, and to have them in their minds, in whose name the images are made. They say, also, that the angels of God speak to them in those idols, and that they do many great miracles. And they say truth, that there is an angel within them; for there are two manner of angels, a good and an evil; as the Greeks say Cacho and Calo. This Cacho is the wicked angel, and Calo is the good angel; but the other is not the good angel, but the wicked angel, which is within the idols to deceive them and maintain them in their error.

There are many other divers countries, and many other marvels beyond, that I have not seen; wherefore I can not speak of them properly. And, also, in the countries where I have been are many diversities of many wonderful things, more than I make mention of; for it were too long a thing to devise you the manner of them all. And therefore now that I have devised you of certain countries, which I have spoken of before, I beseech your worthy and excellent nobleness that it suffice to you at this time; for if I told you all that is beyond the sea, another man, perhaps, who would labor to go into those parts to seek those countries, might be blamed by my words in rehearsing many strange things; for he might not say any thing new, in the which the hearers might have either solace or pleasure.

And you shall understand that, at my coming home, I came to Rome, and showed my life to our Holy Father the Pope, and was absolved of all that lay in my conscience of many divers grievous points, as men must need that are in company, dwelling amongst so many divers people, of divers sects and beliefs, as I have been. And, amongst all I showed him this treatise, that I had made after information of men that knew of things that I had not seen myself; and also of marvels and customs that I had seen myself, as far as God would give me grace; and besought his holy fatherhood that my book might be examined and corrected by advice of his wise and discreet council.

And our Holy Father, of his special grace, gave my book to be examined and proved by the advice of his said council, by the which my book was proved for true, insomuch that they showed me a book, which my book was examined by, that comprehended full much more, by an hundredth part, by the which the *Mappa Mundi* was made. And so my book (albeit that many men list not to give credence to anything but to what they see with their eye, be the author or the person ever so true) is affirmed and proved by our Holy Father in manner and form as I have said.

And I, John Maundeville, knight, above said (although I be unworthy), that went from our countries, and passed the sea, in the year of Grace 1322, have passed many lands, and many isles and countries, and searched many full strange places, and have been in many a full good and honorable company, and at many a fair deed of arms (albeit that I did none myself, from my insufficiency), now I am come home (in spite of myself) to rest; for rheumatic gouts, that distress me, fix the end of my labor, against my will (God knoweth). And thus, taking comfort in my wretched rest, recording the time passed, I have fulfilled these things, and written them in this book, as it would come into my mind, the year of Grace 1356, in the thirty-fourth year that I departed from our country. Wherefore I pray to all the readers and hearers of this book, if it please them, that they would pray to God for me, and I shall pray for them.

THE END.

ADVERTISEMENTS.

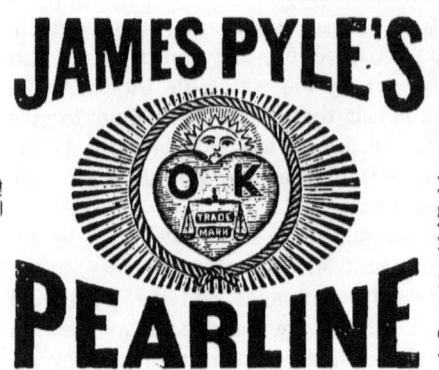

JAMES PYLE'S PEARLINE

THE BEST Washing Compound
EVER INVENTED.

No Lady, Married or Single, Rich or Poor, Housekeeping or Boarding, will be without it after testing its utility.

Sold by all first-class Grocers, but beware of worthless imitations.

ABANDON PHYSIC!
GLUTEN SUPPOSITORIES
CURE CONSTIPATION AND PILES.

50 Cents by Mail.   Circulars Free.

HEALTH FOOD CO.,
4th Avenue and 10th St., N. Y.

CANDY
CANDY

Send $1, $2, $3 or $5 for a sample retail box by Express, of
THE BEST CANDIES IN AMERICA,
put up in elegant boxes, and strictly pure. Suitable for presents. Express charges light. Refer to all Chicago. Try it once.
If preferred, fine candy at 25c., 40c., and 60c. per pound; the best in the land for the money. Address
C. F. GUNTHER,
Confectioner,
CHICAGO.

WHAT IS SAPOLIO?

It is a solid, handsome cake of scouring soap, which has no equal for all cleaning purposes except the laundry. To use it is to value it. What will Sapolio do? Why, it will clean paint, make oil-cloths bright, and give the floors, tables and shelves a new appearance.
It will take the grease off the dishes and off the pots and pans.
You can scour the knives and forks with it, and make the tin things shine brightly. The wash-basin, the bath-tub, even the greasy kitchen sink, will be as clean as a new pin if you use **SAPOLIO.** One cake will prove all we say. Be a clever little housekeeper and try it.

BEWARE OF IMITATIONS.

MUNRO'S PUBLICATIONS.

The Seaside Library---Pocket Edition.

Persons who wish to purchase the following works in complete and unabridged form are cautioned to order and see that they get THE SEASIDE LIBRARY, Pocket Edition, as works published in other Libraries are frequently abridged and incomplete. Every number of THE SEASIDE LIBRARY is unchanged and unabridged.

Newsdealers wishing Catalogues of THE SEASIDE LIBRARY, Pocket Edition, bearing their imprint, will be supplied on sending their names, addresses, and number required.

The works in THE SEASIDE LIBRARY, Pocket Edition, are printed from larger type and on better paper than any other series published.

The following works are for sale by all newsdealers, or will be sent to any address, postage free, on receipt of price, by the publisher. Address
GEORGE MUNRO, Munro's Publishing House,
P. O. Box 3751.   17 to 27 Vandewater Street, N. Y.

[*When ordering by mail please order by numbers.*]

AUTHOR'S LIST.

Works by the author of "Addie's Husband."
388 Addie's Husband; or, Through Clouds to Sunshine............ 10
504 My Poor Wife................. 10

Works by the author of "A Fatal Dower."
246 A Fatal Dower................ 10
372 Phyllis' Probation............ 10
461 His Wedded Wife.............. 20

Works by the author of "A Great Mistake."
244 A Great Mistake.............. 20
588 Cherry....................... 10

Works by the author of "A Woman's Love-Story."
322 A Woman's Love-Story......... 10
677 Griselda..................... 20

Mrs. Alexander's Works.
5 The Admiral's Ward............ 20
17 The Wooing O't............... 20
62 The Executor................. 20
189 Valerie's Fate............... 10
229 Maid, Wife, or Widow?........ 10
236 Which Shall it Be?........... 20
339 Mrs. Vereker's Courier Maid... 10
490 A Second Life................ 20
564 At Bay....................... 10

Alison's Works.
194 "So Near, and Yet So Far!"... 10
278 For Life and Love............ 10
481 The House That Jack Built.... 10

F. Anstey's Works.
59 Vice Versâ................... 20
225 The Giant's Robe............. 20
503 The Tinted Venus. A Farcical Romance....................... 10

R. M. Ballantyne's Works.
89 The Red Eric................. 10
95 The Fire Brigade............. 10
96 Erling the Bold.............. 10

Anne Beale's Works.
188 Idonea....................... 20
199 The Fisher Village........... 10

Basil's Works.
344 "The Wearing of the Green".. 20
547 A Coquette's Conquest........ 20
585 A Drawn Game................. 20

M. Betham-Edwards's Works.
273 Love and Mirage; or, The Waiting on an Island............ 10
579 The Flower of Doom, and Other Stories....................... 10
594 Doctor Jacob................. 20

Walter Besant's Works.
97 All in a Garden Fair......... 20
137 Uncle Jack................... 10
140 A Glorious Fortune........... 10
146 Love Finds the Way, and Other Stories. By Besant and Rice 10
230 Dorothy Forster.............. 20
324 In Luck at Last.............. 10
651 "Self or Bearer"............. 10

William Black's Works.
1 Yolande...................... 20
18 Shandon Bells................ 20
21 Sunrise: A Story of These Times........................ 20
23 A Princess of Thule.......... 20
39 In Silk Attire............... 20
44 Macleod of Dare.............. 20
49 That Beautiful Wretch........ 20
50 The Strange Adventures of a Phaeton...................... 20
70 White Wings: A Yachting Romance......................... 10

(1)

THE SEASIDE LIBRARY.—Pocket Edition.

William Black's Works—Continued.

78 Madcap Violet	20
81 A Daughter of Heth	20
124 Three Feathers	20
125 The Monarch of Mincing Lane.	20
126 Kilmeny	20
138 Green Pastures and Piccadilly.	20
265 Judith Shakespeare: Her Love Affairs and Other Adventures	20
472 The Wise Women of Inverness.	10
627 White Heather	20

R. D. Blackmore's Works.

67 Lorna Doone. 1st half	20
67 Lorna Doone. 2d half	20
427 The Remarkable History of Sir Thomas Upmore, Bart., M. P.	20
615 Mary Anerley	20
625 Erema; or, My Father's Sin	20
629 Cripps, the Carrier	20
630 Cradock Nowell. First half	20
630 Cradock Nowell. Second half.	20
631 Christowell. A Dartmoor Tale	20
632 Clara Vaughan	20
633 The Maid of Sker. First half	20
633 The Maid of Sker. Second half	20
636 Alice Lorraine. First half	20
636 Alice Lorraine. Second half	20

Miss M. E. Braddon's Works.

35 Lady Audley's Secret	20
58 Phantom Fortune	20
74 Aurora Floyd	20
110 Under the Red Flag	10
153 The Golden Calf	20
204 Vixen	20
211 The Octoroon	10
234 Barbara; or, Splendid Misery..	20
263 An Ishmaelite	20
315 The Mistletoe Bough. Edited by Miss Braddon	20
434 Wyllard's Weird	20
478 Diavola; or, Nobody's Daughter. Part I	20
478 Diavola; or, Nobody's Daughter. Part II	20
480 Married in Haste. Edited by Miss M. E. Braddon	20
487 Put to the Test. Edited by Miss M. E. Braddon	20
488 Joshua Haggard's Daughter	20
489 Rupert Godwin	20
495 Mount Royal	20
496 Only a Woman. Edited by Miss M. E. Braddon	20
497 The Lady's Mile	20
498 Only a Clod	20
499 The Cloven Foot	20
511 A Strange World	20
515 Sir Jasper's Tenant	20
524 Strangers and Pilgrims	20
529 The Doctor's Wife	20
542 Fenton's Quest	20
544 Cut by the County; or, Grace Darnel	10
548 The Fatal Marriage, and The Shadow in the Corner	10
549 Dudley Carleon; or, The Brother's Secret, and George Caulfield's Journey	10
552 Hostages to Fortune	20
553 Birds of Prey	20
554 Charlotte's Inheritance. (Sequel to "Birds of Prey")	20
557 To the Bitter End	20
559 Taken at the Flood	20
560 Asphodel	20
561 Just as I am; or, A Living Lie	20
567 Dead Men's Shoes	20
570 John Marchmont's Legacy.	20
618 The Mistletoe Bough. Christmas, 1885. Edited by Miss M. E. Braddon	20

Works by Charlotte M. Braeme, Author of "Dora Thorne."

19 Her Mother's Sin	10
51 Dora Thorne	20
54 A Broken Wedding-Ring	20
68 A Queen Amongst Women	10
69 Madolin's Lover	20
73 Redeemed by Love	20
76 Wife in Name Only	20
79 Wedded and Parted	10
92 Lord Lynne's Choice	10
148 Thorns and Orange-Blossoms	10
190 Romance of a Black Veil	10
220 Which Loved Him Best?	10
237 Repented at Leisure	20
249 "Prince Charlie's Daughter"	10
250 Sunshine and Roses; or, Diana's Discipline	10
254 The Wife's Secret, and Fair but False	10
283 The Sin of a Lifetime	10
287 At War With Herself	10
288 From Gloom to Sunlight	10
291 Love's Warfare	10
292 A Golden Heart	10
293 The Shadow of a Sin	10
294 Hilda	10
295 A Woman's War	10
296 A Rose in Thorns	10
297 Hilary's Folly	10
299 The Fatal Lilies, and A Bride from the Sea	10
300 A Gilded Sin, and A Bridge of Love	10
303 Ingledew House, and More Bitter than Death	10
304 In Cupid's Net	10
305 A Dead Heart, and Lady Gwendoline's Dream	10
306 A Golden Dawn, and Love for a Day	10
307 Two Kisses, and Like no Other Love	10
308 Beyond Pardon	20
411 A Bitter Atonement	20
433 My Sister Kate	20
459 A Woman's Temptation	20
460 Under a Shadow	20
465 The Earl's Atonement	20
466 Between Two Loves	20
467 A Struggle for a Ring	20

(2)

THE SEASIDE LIBRARY.—*Pocket Edition.*

Works by Charlotte M. Braeme—Continued.
- 469 Lady Damer's Secret........... 20
- 470 Evelyn's Folly................ 20
- 471 Thrown on the World......... 20
- 476 Between Two Sins............. 10
- 516 Put Asunder; or, Lady Castlemaine's Divorce............. 20
- 576 Her Martyrdom................ 20
- 626 A Fair Mystery................ 20
- 741 The Heiress of Hilldrop; or, The Romance of a Young Girl........................ 20
- 745 For Another's Sin; or, A Struggle for Love................. 20

Charlotte Bronte's Works.
- 15 Jane Eyre..................... 20
- 57 Shirley....................... 20

Rhoda Broughton's Works.
- 86 Belinda....................... 20
- 101 Second Thoughts............... 20
- 227 Nancy........................ 20
- 645 Mrs. Smith of Longmains...... 10

Robert Buchanan's Works.
- 145 "Storm-Beaten:" God and The Man......................... 20
- 154 Annan Water.................. 20
- 181 The New Abelard.............. 10
- 398 Matt: A Tale of a Caravan.... 10
- 646 The Master of the Mine....... 10
- 647 Goblin Gold.................. 10

Captain Fred Burnaby's Works.
- 375 A Ride to Khiva.............. 20
- 384 On Horseback Through Asia Minor....................... 20

E. Fairfax Byrrne's Works.
- 521 Entangled.................... 20
- 538 A Fair Country Maid.......... 20

Hall Caine's Works.
- 445 The Shadow of a Crime........ 20
- 520 She's All the World to Me.... 10

Rosa Nouchette Carey's Works.
- 215 Not Like Other Girls......... 20
- 396 Robert Ord's Atonement....... 20
- 551 Barbara Heathcote's Trial.... 20
- 608 For Lilias................... 20

Wilkie Collins's Works.
- 52 The New Magdalen.............. 10
- 102 The Moonstone................ 20
- 167 Heart and Science............ 20
- 168 No Thoroughfare. By Dickens and Collins................. 10
- 175 Love's Random Shot........... 10
- 233 "I Say No;" or, The Love-Letter Answered................. 20
- 508 The Girl at the Gate......... 10
- 591 The Queen of Hearts.......... 20
- 613 The Ghost's Touch, and Percy and the Prophet............ 10
- 623 My Lady's Money.............. 20
- 701 The Woman in White. 1st half 20

- 701 The Woman in White. 2d half 20
- 702 Man and Wife. 1st half...... 20
- 702 Man and Wife. 2d half....... 20

Hugh Conway's Works.
- 240 Called Back.................. 10
- 251 The Daughter of the Stars, and Other Tales................ 10
- 301 Dark Days.................... 10
- 302 The Blatchford Bequest....... 10
- 502 Carriston's Gift............. 10
- 525 Paul Vargas, and Other Stories 10
- 543 A Family Affair.............. 20
- 601 Slings and Arrows, and Other Stories..................... 10
- 711 A Cardinal Sin............... 20

J. Fenimore Cooper's Works.
- 60 The Last of the Mohicans..... 20
- 63 The Spy...................... 20
- 309 The Pathfinder............... 20
- 310 The Prairie.................. 20
- 318 The Pioneers; or, The Sources of the Susquehanna......... 20
- 349 The Two Admirals............. 20
- 359 The Water-Witch.............. 20
- 361 The Red Rover................ 20
- 373 Wing and Wing................ 20
- 378 Homeward Bound; or, The Chase....................... 20
- 379 Home as Found. (Sequel to "Homeward Bound").......... 20
- 380 Wyandotte; or, The Hutted Knoll....................... 20
- 385 The Headsman; or, The Abbaye des Vignerons.......... 20
- 394 The Bravo.................... 20
- 397 Lionel Lincoln; or, The Leaguer of Boston............... 20
- 400 The Wept of Wish-Ton-Wish... 20
- 413 Afloat and Ashore............ 20
- 414 Miles Wallingford. (Sequel to "Afloat and Ashore")....... 20
- 415 The Ways of the Hour......... 20
- 416 Jack Tier; or, The Florida Reef 20
- 419 The Chainbearer; or, The Littlepage Manuscripts............ 20
- 420 Satanstoe; or, The Littlepage Manuscripts................ 20
- 421 The Redskins; or, Indian and Injin. Being the conclusion of the Littlepage Manuscripts 20
- 422 Precaution................... 20
- 423 The Sea Lions; or, The Lost Sealers..................... 20
- 424 Mercedes of Castile; or, The Voyage to Cathay........... 20
- 425 The Oak-Openings; or, The Bee-Hunter..................... 20
- 431 The Monikins................. 20

Georgiana M. Craik's Works.
- 450 Godfrey Helstone............. 20
- 606 Mrs. Hollyer................. 20

B. M. Croker's Works.
- 207 Pretty Miss Neville.......... 20
- 260 Proper Pride................. 10
- 412 Some One Else................ 20

(3)

May Crommelin's Works.

- 452 In the West Countrie........... 20
- 619 Joy; or, The Light of Coldhome Ford................... 20

Alphonse Daudet's Works.

- 534 Jack........................:.... 20
- 574 The Nabob: A Story of Parisian Life and Manners............ 20

Charles Dickens's Works.

- 10 The Old Curiosity Shop........ 20
- 22 David Copperfield. Vol. I..... 20
- 22 David Copperfield. Vol. II.... 20
- 24 Pickwick Papers. Vol. I....... 20
- 24 Pickwick Papers. Vol. II...... 20
- 37 Nicholas Nickleby. First half. 20
- 37 Nicholas Nickleby. Second half 20
- 41 Oliver Twist..................... 20
- 77 A Tale of Two Cities............ 20
- 84 Hard Times..................... 10
- 91 Barnaby Rudge. 1st half...... 20
- 91 Barnaby Rudge. 2d half...... 20
- 94 Little Dorrit. First half....... 20
- 94 Little Dorrit. Second half..... 20
- 106 Bleak House. First half....... 20
- 106 Bleak House. Second half.... 20
- 107 Dombey and Son. 1st half 20
- 107 Dombey and Son. 2d half..... 20
- 108 The Cricket on the Hearth, and Doctor Marigold............... 10
- 131 Our Mutual Friend. (1st half). 20
- 131 Our Mutual Friend. (2d half).. 20
- 132 Master Humphrey's Clock..... 10
- 152 The Uncommercial Traveler... 20
- 168 No Thoroughfare. By Dickens and Collins................... 10
- 169 The Haunted Man............... 10
- 437 Life and Adventures of Martin Chuzzlewit. First half....... 20
- 437 Life and Adventures of Martin Chuzzlewit. Second half..... 20
- 439 Great Expectations............ 20
- 440 Mrs. Lirriper's Lodgings...... 10
- 447 American Notes................ 20
- 448 Pictures From Italy, and The Mudfog Papers, &c........... 20
- 454 The Mystery of Edwin Drood.. 20
- 456 Sketches by Boz. Illustrative of Every-day Life and Everyday People................... 20
- 676 A Child's History of England.. 20

F. Du Boisgobey's Works.

- 82 Sealed Lips..................... 20
- 104 The Coral Pin. 1st half........ 20
- 104 The Coral Pin. 2d half........ 20
- 264 Piédouche, a French Detective. 10
- 328 Babiole, the Pretty Milliner. First half..................... 20
- 328 Babiole, the Pretty Milliner. Second half................. 20
- 453 The Lottery Ticket............. 20
- 475 The Prima Donna's Husband., 20
- 522 Zig-Zag, the Clown; or, Steel Gauntlets..................... 20
- 523 The Consequences of a Duel. A Parisian Romance............ 20

- 648 The Angel of the Bells......... 20
- 697 The Pretty Jailer. 1st half.... 20
- 697 The Pretty Jailer. 2d half..... 20
- 699 The Sculptor's Daughter. 1st half........................... 20
- 699 The Sculptor's Daughter. 2d half........................... 20

"The Duchess's" Works.

- 2 Molly Bawn.................... 20
- 6 Portia.......................... 20
- 14 Airy Fairy Lilian.............. 10
- 16 Phyllis......................... 20
- 25 Mrs. Geoffrey.................. 20
- 29 Beauty's Daughters............ 10
- 30 Faith and Unfaith.............. 20
- 118 Loys, Lord Berresford, and Eric Dering................... 10
- 119 Monica, and A Rose Distill'd... 10
- 123 Sweet is True Love............ 10
- 129 Rossmoyne..................... 10
- 134 The Witching Hour, and Other Stories........................ 10
- 136 "That Last Rehearsal," and Other Stories................. 10
- 166 Moonshine and Marguerites.... 10
- 171 Fortune's Wheel............... 10
- 284 Doris........................... 10
- 312 A Week in Killarney........... 10
- 342 The Baby, and One New Year's Eve............................ 10
- 390 Mildred Trevanion............. 10
- 404 In Durance Vile, and Other Stories........................ 10
- 486 Dick's Sweetheart.............. 10
- 494 A Maiden All Forlorn, and Barbara......................... 10
- 517 A Passive Crime, and Other Stories........................ 10
- 541 "As It Fell Upon a Day.".... 10
- 733 Lady Branksmere.............. 10

Alexander Dumas's Works.

- 55 The Three Guardsmen......... 20
- 75 Twenty Years After............ 20
- 259 The Bride of Monte-Cristo. A Sequel to "The Count of Monte-Cristo"................ 10
- 262 The Count of Monte-Cristo. Part I......................... 20
- 262 The Count of Monte-Cristo. Part II........................ 20
- 717 Beau Tancrede; or, The Marriage Verdict................. 20

George Eliot's Works.

- 3 The Mill on the Floss.......... 20
- 36 Adam Bede..................... 20
- 31 Middlemarch. 1st half......... 20
- 31 Middlemarch. 2d half......... 20
- 34 Daniel Deronda. 1st half..... 20
- 34 Daniel Deronda. 2d half..... 20
- 42 Romola......................... 20
- 693 Felix Holt, the Radical........ 20
- 707 Silas Marner: The Weaver of Raveloe....................... 10
- 728 Janet's Repentance............ 10

(4)

THE SEASIDE LIBRARY.—Pocket Edition.

B. L. Farjeon's Works.
179 Little Make-Believe............ 10
573 Love's Harvest 20
607 Self-Doomed................. 10
616 The Sacred Nugget............ 20
657 Christmas Angel............. 10

G. Manville Fenn's Works.
193 The Rosery Folk.............. 10
558 Poverty Corner............... 20
587 The Parson o' Dumford........ 20
609 The Dark House............... 10

Octave Feuillet's Works.
66 The Romance of a Poor Young Man......................... 10
386 Led Astray; or, "La Petite Comtesse".................... 10

Mrs. Forrester's Works.
80 June........................ 20
280 Omnia Vanitas. A Tale of Society......................... 10
484 Although He Was a Lord, and Other Tales.................. 10
715 I Have Lived and Loved....... 20
721 Dolores...................... 20
724 My Lord and My Lady......... 20
726 My Hero..................... 20
727 Fair Women.................. 20
729 Mignon...................... 20
732 From Olympus to Hades....... 20
734 Viva........................ 20
736 Roy and Viola................ 20
740 Rhona....................... 20
744 Diana Carew; or, For a Woman's Sake..................... 20

Jessie Fothergill's Works.
314 Peril........................ 20
572 Healey...................... 20

R. E. Francillon's Works.
135 A Great Heiress: A Fortune in Seven Checks.............. 10
319 Face to Face: A Fact in Seven Fables....................... 10
360 Ropes of Sand................ 20
656 The Golden Flood. By R. E. Francillon and Wm. Senior.. 10
656 The Golden Flood. By R. E. Francillon and Wm. Senior.. 10

Emile Gaboriau's Works.
7 File No. 113................. 20
12 Other People's Money......... 20
20 Within an Inch of His Life.... 20
26 Monsieur Lecoq. Vol I....... 20
26 Monsieur Lecoq. Vol. II..... 20
33 The Clique of Gold............ 10
38 The Widow Lerouge........... 20
43 The Mystery of Orcival....... 20
144 Promises of Marriage......... 10

Charles Gibbon's Works.
64 A Maiden Fair................ 10
317 By Mead and Stream.......... 20

Miss Grant's Works.
222 The Sun-Maid................ 20
555 Cara Roma................... 20

Arthur Griffiths's Works.
614 No. 99....................... 10
680 Fast and Loose............... 20

Thomas Hardy's Works.
139 The Romantic Adventures of a Milkmaid................... 10
530 A Pair of Blue Eyes........... 20
690 Far From the Madding Crowd. 20

John B. Harwood's Works.
143 One False, Both Fair.......... 20
358 Within the Clasp............. 20

Mary Cecil Hay's Works.
65 Back to the Old Home......... 10
72 Old Myddelton's Money....... 20
196 Hidden Perils................ 10
197 For Her Dear Sake............ 20
224 The Arundel Motto........... 20
281 The Squire's Legacy.......... 20
290 Nora's Love Test.............. 20
408 Lester's Secret............... 20
678 Dorothy's Venture............ 20
716 Victor and Vanquished........ 20

Tighe Hopkins's Works.
509 Nell Haffenden.............. 20
714 'Twixt Love and Duty........ 20

Works by the Author of "Judith Wynne."
332 Judith Wynne................ 20
506 Lady Lovelace............... 20

William H. G. Kingston's Works.
117 A Tale of the Shore and Ocean. 20
133 Peter the Whaler............. 10

Charles Lever's Works.
191 Harry Lorrequer............. 20
212 Charles O'Malley, the Irish Dragoon. First half............. 20
212 Charles O'Malley, the Irish Dragoon. Second half........... 20
243 Tom Burke of "Ours." First half........................ 20
243 Tom Burke of "Ours." Second half....................... 20

Mary Linskill's Works.
473 A Lost Son................... 20
620 Between the Heather and the Northern Sea................. 20

Samuel Lover's Works.
663 Handy Andy.................. 20
664 Rory O'More................. 20

Sir E. Bulwer Lytton's Works.
40 The Last Days of Pompeii..... 20
83 A Strange Story.............. 20
90 Ernest Maltravers............ 20
130 The Last of the Barons. First half........................ 20
130 The Last of the Barons. Second half....................... 20
162 Eugene Aram................. 20
164 Leila; or, The Siege of Grenada 10
650 Alice; or, The Mysteries. (A Sequel to "Ernest Maltravers") 20
720 Paul Clifford................. 20

(5)

THE SEASIDE LIBRARY.—Pocket Edition.

George Macdonald's Works.
282 Donal Grant.................... 20
325 The Portent................... 10
326 Phantastes. A Faerie Romance for Men and Women......... 10
722 What's Mine's Mine............ 20

Florence Marryat's Works.
159 A Moment of Madness, and Other Stories............... 10
183 Old Contrairy, and Other Stories....................... 10
208 The Ghost of Charlotte Cray, and Other Stories........... 10
276 Under the Lilies and Roses.... 10
444 The Heart of Jane Warner..... 20
449 Peeress and Player............ 20
689 The Heir Presumptive......... 20

Captain Marryat's Works.
88 The Privateersman............ 20
272 The Little Savage............. 10

Helen B. Mathers's Works.
13 Eyre's Acquittal............... 10
221 Comin' Thro' the Rye......... 20
438 Found Out.................... 10
535 Murder or Manslaughter?..... 10
673 Story of a Sin................. 20
713 "Cherry Ripe"................. 20

Justin McCarthy's Works.
121 Maid of Athens................ 20
602 Camiola...................... 20
685 England Under Gladstone. 1880—1885................. 20
747 Our Sensation Novel. Edited by Justin H. McCarthy, M.P.. 10

Mrs. Alex. McVeigh Miller's Works.
267 Laurel Vane; or, The Girls' Conspiracy................. 20
268 Lady Gay's Pride; or, The Miser's Treasure............ 20
269 Lancaster's Choice............ 20
316 Sworn to Silence; or, Aline Rodney's Secret............ 20

Jean Middlemas's Works.
155 Lady Muriel's Secret.......... 20
539 Silvermead................... 20

Alan Muir's Works.
172 "Golden Girls"................ 20
346 Tumbledown Farm............ 10

Miss Mulock's Works.
11 John Halifax, Gentleman...... 20
245 Miss Tommy.................. 10

David Christie Murray's Works.
58 By the Gate of the Sea........ 10
195 "The Way of the World"...... 20
320 A Bit of Human Nature....... 10
661 Rainbow Gold................. 20
674 First Person Singular......... 20
691 Valentine Strange............. 20
695 Hearts: Queen, Knave, and Deuce....................... 20
698 A Life's Atonement............ 20
737 Aunt Rachel.................. 10

Works by the author of "My Ducats and My Daughter."
376 The Crime of Christmas Day. 10
596 My Ducats and My Daughter... 20

W. E. Norris's Works.
184 Thirlby Hall.................. 20
277 A Man of His Word........... 10
355 That Terrible Man............ 10
500 Adrian Vidal.................. 20

Laurence Oliphant's Works.
47 Altiora Peto................... 20
537 Piccadilly..................... 10

Mrs. Oliphant's Works.
45 A Little Pilgrim............... 10
177 Salem Chapel................. 20
205 The Minister's Wife........... 30
321 The Prodigals, and Their Inheritance................... 10
337 Memoirs and Resolutions of Adam Graeme of Mossgray, including some Chronicles of the Borough of Fendie...... 20
345 Madam....................... 20
351 The House on the Moor....... 20
357 John......................... 20
370 Lucy Crofton................. 10
371 Margaret Maitland............ 20
377 Magdalen Hepburn: A Story of the Scottish Reformation.... 20
402 Lilliesleaf; or, Passages in the Life of Mrs. Margaret Maitland of Sunnyside............ 20
410 Old Lady Mary................ 10
527 The Days of My Life........... 20
528 At His Gates.................. 20
568 The Perpetual Curate......... 20
569 Harry Muir................... 20
603 Agnes. 1st half............... 20
603 Agnes. 2d half............... 20
604 Innocent. 1st half............ 20
604 Innocent. 2d half............ 20
605 Ombra....................... 20
645 Oliver's Bride................ 10
655 The Open Door, and The Portrait........................ 10
687 A Country Gentleman......... 20
703 A House Divided Against Itself 20
710 The Greatest Heiress in England 20

"Ouida's" Works.
4 Under Two Flags.............. 20
9 Wanda, Countess von Szalras.. 20
116 Moths........................ 20
128 Afternoon and Other Sketches. 10
226 Friendship.................... 20
228 Princess Napraxine........... 20
238 Pascarel...................... 20
239 Signa......................... 20
433 A Rainy June................. 10
639 Othmar....................... 20
671 Don Gesualdo................. 10
672 In Maremma. First half..... 20
672 In Maremma. Second half.... 20

James Payn's Works.

48 Thicker Than Water 20
186 The Canon's Ward 20
343 The Talk of the Town 20
577 In Peril and Privation 10
589 The Luck of the Darrells 20

Miss Jane Porter's Works.

660 The Scottish Chiefs. 1st half.. 20
660 The Scottish Chiefs. 2d half.. 20
696 Thaddeus of Warsaw 20

Cecil Power's Works.

336 Philistia 20
611 Babylon 20

Mrs. Campbell Praed's Works.

428 Zéro: A Story of Monte-Carlo. 10
477 Affinities 10

Eleanor C. Price's Works.

173 The Foreigners 20
331 Gerald 20

Charles Reade's Works.

46 Very Hard Cash 20
98 A Woman-Hater 20
206 The Picture, and Jack of All Trades 10
210 Readiana: Comments on Current Events 10
213 A Terrible Temptation 20
214 Put Yourself in His Place 20
216 Foul Play 20
231 Griffith Gaunt; or, Jealousy .. 20
232 Love and Money; or, A Perilous Secret 10
235 "It is Never Too Late to Mend." A Matter-of-Fact Romance 20

Mrs. J. H. Riddell's Works.

71 A Struggle for Fame 20
593 Berna Boyle 20

"Rita's" Works.

252 A Sinless Secret 10
446 Dame Durden 20
598 "Corinna." A Study 10
617 Like Dian's Kiss 20

F. W. Robinson's Works.

157 Milly's Hero 20
217 The Man She Cared For 20
261 A Fair Maid 20
455 Lazarus in London 20
590 The Courting of Mary Smith .. 20

W. Clark Russell's Works.

85 A Sea Queen 20
109 Little Loo 20
180 Round the Galley Fire 10
209 John Holdsworth, Chief Mate.. 10
223 A Sailor's Sweetheart 20
592 A Strange Voyage 20
682 In the Middle Watch. Sea Stories 20
743 Jack's Courtship. 1st half.... 20
743 Jack's Courtship. 2d half,.... 20

Sir Walter Scott's Works.

28 Ivanhoe 20
201 The Monastery 20
202 The Abbot. (Sequel to "The Monastery") 20
353 The Black Dwarf, and A Legend of Montrose 20
362 The Bride of Lammermoor.... 20
363 The Surgeon's Daughter 10
364 Castle Dangerous 10
391 The Heart of Mid-Lothian 20
392 Peveril of the Peak 20
393 The Pirate 20
401 Waverley 20
417 The Fair Maid of Perth; or, St. Valentine's Day 20
418 St. Ronan's Well 20
463 Redgauntlet. A Tale of the Eighteenth Century 20
507 Chronicles of the Canongate, and Other Stories 10

William Sime's Works.

429 Boulderstone; or, New Men and Old Populations 10
580 The Red Route 20
597 Haco the Dreamer 10
649 Cradle and Spade 20

Hawley Smart's Works.

348 From Post to Finish. A Racing Romance 20
367 Tie and Trick 20
550 Struck Down 10

Frank E. Smedley's Works.

333 Frank Fairlegh; or, Scenes from the Life of a Private Pupil 20
562 Lewis Arundel; or, The Railroad of Life 20

T. W. Speight's Works.

150 For Himself Alone 10
653 A Barren Title 10

Robert Louis Stevenson's Works.

686 Strange Case of Dr. Jekyll and Mr. Hyde 10
704 Prince Otto 10

Julian Sturgis's Works.

405 My Friends and I. Edited by Julian Sturgis 10
694 John Maidment 20

Eugene Sue's Works.

270 The Wandering Jew. Part I... 20
270 The Wandering Jew. Part II.. 20
271 The Mysteries of Paris. Part I. 20
271 The Mysteries of Paris. Part II. 20

George Temple's Works.

599 Lancelot Ward, M.P. 10
642 Britta 10

(7)

THE SEASIDE LIBRARY.—Pocket Edition.

William M. Thackeray's Works.
27 Vanity Fair........................... 20
165 The History of Henry Esmond. 20
464 The Newcomes. Part I........ 20
464 The Newcomes. Part II....... 20
531 The Prime Minister (1st half).. 20
531 The Prime Minister (2d half).. 20
670 The Rose and the Ring. Illustrated....................... 10

Annie Thomas's Works.
141 She Loved Him!.............. 10
142 Jenifer........................ 20
565 No Medium.................... 10

Anthony Trollope's Works.
32 The Land Leaguers........... 20
93 Anthony Trollope's Autobiography....................... 20
147 Rachel Ray................... 20
200 An Old Man's Love........... 10
531 The Prime Minister. 1st half.. 20
531 The Prime Minister. 2d half... 20
621 The Warden................... 10
622 Harry Heathcote of Gangoil... 10
667 The Golden Lion of Granpere.. 20
700 Ralph the Heir. 1st half...... 20
700 Ralph the Heir. 2d half....... 20

Margaret Veley's Works.
298 Mitchelhurst Place............ 10
586 " For Percival "............... 20

Jules Verne's Works.
87 Dick Sand; or, A Captain at Fifteen..................... 20
100 20,000 Leagues Under the Seas. 20
368 The Southern Star; or, the Diamond Land................. 20
395 The Archipelago on Fire...... 10
578 Mathias Sandorf. Illustrated. Part I...................... 10
578 Mathias Sandorf. Illustrated. Part II..................... 10
578 Mathias Sandorf. Illustrated. Part III.................... 20
659 The Waif of the "Cynthia"... 20

L. B. Walford's Works.
241 The Baby's Grandmother...... 10
256 Mr. Smith: A Part of His Life. 20
258 Cousins....................... 20
658 The History of a Week........ 10

F. Warden's Works.
192 At the World's Mercy......... 20
248 The House on the Marsh...... 10
286 Deldee; or, The Iron Hand.... 20
482 A Vagrant Wife............... 20
556 A Prince of Darkness......... 20

E. Werner's Works.
327 Raymond's Atonement........ 20
540 At a High Price............... 20

G. J. Whyte-Melville's Works.
409 Roy's Wife................... 20
451 Market Harborough, and Inside the Bar....................... 20

John Strange Winter's Works.
492 Mignon; or, Bootles' Baby. Illustrated................... 10
600 Houp-La. Illustrated........ 10
638 In Quarters with the 25th (The Black Horse) Dragoons...... 10
688 A Man of Honor. Illustrated.. 10
746 Cavalry Life; or, Sketches and Stories in Barracks and Out.. 20

Mrs. Henry Wood's Works.
8 East Lynne.................... 20
255 The Mystery.................. 20
277 The Surgeon's Daughters...... 10
508 The Unholy Wish............. 10
513 Helen Whitney's Wedding, and Other Tales................ 10
514 The Mystery of Jessy Page, and Other Tales................ 10
610 The Story of Dorothy Grape, and Other Tales............. 10

Charlotte M. Yonge's Works.
247 The Armourer's Prentices..... 10
275 The Three Brides............. 10
535 Henrietta's Wish. A Tale..... 10
563 The Two Sides of the Shield.... 20
640 Nuttie's Father............... 20
665 The Dove in the Eagle's Nest.. 20
666 My Young Alcides: A Faded Photograph.................. 20
739 The Caged Lion............... 20
742 Love and Life................. 20

Miscellaneous.
53 The Story of Ida. Francesca.. 10
61 Charlotte Temple. Mrs. Rowson........................ 10
99 Barbara's History. Amelia B. Edwards.................... 20
103 Rose Fleming. Dora Russell.. 10
105 A Noble Wife. John Saunders 20
111 The Little School-master Mark. J. H. Shorthouse............ 10
112 The Waters of Marah. John Hill......................... 20
113 Mrs. Carr's Companion. M. G. Wightwick.................. 10
114 Some of Our Girls. Mrs. C. J. Eiloart...................... 20
115 Diamond Cut Diamond. T. Adolphus Trollope........... 10
120 Tom Brown's School Days at Rugby. Thomas Hughes.... 20
122 Ione Stewart. Mrs. E. Lynn Linton...................... 20
127 Adrian Bright. Mrs. Caddy.... 20
149 The Captain's Daughter. From the Russian of Pushkin...... 10
151 The Ducie Diamonds. C. Blatherwick..................... 10

Miscellaneous—Continued.

156 "For a Dream's Sake." Mrs. Herbert Martin............... 20
158 The Starling. Norman Macleod, D.D.................... 10
160 Her Gentle Deeds. Sarah Tytler...................... 10
161 The Lady of Lyons. Founded on the Play of that title by Lord Lytton.................. 10
163 Winifred Power. Joyce Darrell....................... 20
170 A Great Treason. Mary Hoppus....................... 30
174 Under a Ban. Mrs. Lodge..... 20
176 An April Day. Philippa Prittie Jephson................. 10
178 More Leaves from the Journal of a Life in the Highlands. Queen Victoria............... 10
182 The Millionaire............... 20
185 Dita. Lady Margaret Majendie 10
187 The Midnight Sun. Fredrika Bremer...................... 10
198 A Husband's Story........... 10
203 John Bull and His Island. Max O'Rell....................... 10
218 Agnes Sorel. G. P. R. James.. 20
219 Lady Clare: or, The Master of the Forges. From French of Georges Ohnet............... 10
242 The Two Orphans. D'Ennery. 10
253 The Amazon. Carl Vosmaer... 10
257 Beyond Recall. Adeline Sergeant...................... 10
266 The Water-Babies. Rev. Chas. Kingsley.................... 10
274 Alice, Grand Duchess of Hesse, Princess of Great Britain and Ireland. Biographical Sketch and Letters................. 10
279 Little Goldie: A Story of Woman's Love. Mrs. Sumner Hayden......................... 20
285 The Gambler's Wife.......... 20
289 John Bull's Neighbor in Her True Light. A "Brutal Saxon"....................... 10
311 Two Years Before the Mast. R. H. Dana, Jr................. 20
313 The Lover's Creed. Mrs. Cashel Hoey.................... 20
323 A Willful Maid............... 20
329 The Polish Jew. (Translated from the French by Caroline A. Merighi.) Erckmann-Chatrian....................... 10
330 May Blossom; or, Between Two Loves. Margaret Lee......... 20
334 A Marriage of Convenience. Harriett Jay................. 10
335 The White Witch............. 20
338 The Family Difficulty. Sarah Doudney.................... 10
340 Under Which King? Compton Reade....................... 20
441 Madolin Rivers; or, The Little Beauty of Red Oak Seminary. Laura Jean Libbey........... 20

347 As Avon Flows. Henry Scott Vince....................... 20
350 Diana of the Crossways. George Meredith................... 10
352 At Any Cost. Edward Garrett. 10
354 The Lottery of Life. A Story of New York Twenty Years Ago. John Brougham...... 20
355 The Princess Dagomar of Poland. Heinrich Felbermann. 10
356 A Good Hater. Frederick Boyle 20
365 George Christy; or, The Fortunes of a Minstrel. Tony Pastor...................... 20
366 The Mysterious Hunter; or, The Man of Death. Capt. L. C. Carleton.................. 20
369 Miss Bretherton. Mrs. Humphry Ward................. 10
374 The Dead Man's Secret. Dr. Jupiter Paeon................ 20
381 The Red Cardinal. Frances Elliot....................... 10
382 Three Sisters. Elsa D'Esterre-Keeling..................... 10
383 Introduced to Society. Hamilton Aïdé.................... 10
387 The Secret of the Cliffs. Charlotte French................. 20
389 Ichabod. A Portrait. Bertha Thomas..................... 10
399 Miss Brown. Vernon Lee..... 20
403 An English Squire. C. R. Coleridge...................... 20
406 The Merchant's Clerk. Samuel Warren..................... 10
407 Tylney Hall. Thomas Hood... 20
426 Venus's Doves. Ida Ashworth Taylor..................... 20
430 A Bitter Reckoning. Author of "By Crooked Paths".... 10
432 The Witch's Head. H. Rider Haggard.................... 20
435 Klytia: A Story of Heidelberg Castle. George Taylor....... 20
436 Stella. Fanny Lewald........ 20
441 A Sea Change. Flora L. Shaw. 20
442 Ranthorpe. George Henry Lewes...................... 20
443 The Bachelor of the Albany... 10
457 The Russians at the Gates of Herat. Charles Marvin...... 10
458 A Week of Passion; or, The Dilemma of Mr. George Barton the Younger. Edward Jenkins..................... 20
462 Alice's Adventures in Wonderland. By Lewis Carroll. With forty-two illustrations by John Tenniel...............20
468 The Fortunes, Good and Bad, of a Sewing-Girl. Charlotte M. Stanley.................. 10
474 Serapis. An Historical Novel. George Ebers............... 20
479 Louisa. Katharine S. Macquoid 20
483 Betwixt My Love and Me...... 10
485 Tinted Vapours. J. Maclaren Cobban..................... 10

THE SEASIDE LIBRARY.—Pocket Edition.

Miscellaneous—Continued.

491 Society in London. A Foreign Resident... 10
493 Colonel Enderby's Wife. Lucas Malet... 20
501 Mr. Butler's Ward. F. Mabel Robinson... 20
510 A Mad Love. Author of "Lover and Lord"... 10
512 The Waters of Hercules... 20
504 Curly: An Actor's Story. John Coleman... 10
505 The Society of London. Count Paul Vasili... 10
509 Nell Haffenden. Tighe Hopkins 20
518 The Hidden Sin... 20
519 James Gordon's Wife... 20
526 Madame De Presnel. E. Frances Poynter... 20
532 Arden Court. Barbara Graham 20
536 Dissolving Views. By Mrs. Andrew Lang... 10
545 Vida's Story. By the author of "Guilty Without Crime"... 10
546 Mrs. Keith's Crime. A Novel.. 10
533 Hazel Kirke. Marie Walsh.... 20
566 The Royal Highlanders; or, The Black Watch in Egypt. James Grant... 20
571 Paul Crew's Story. Alice Comyns Carr... 10
575 The Finger of Fate. Captain Mayne Reid... 20
581 The Betrothed. (I Promessi Sposi.) Allessandro Manzoni 20
582 Lucia, Hugh and Another. Mrs. J. H. Needell... 20
583 Victory Deane. Cecil Griffith.. 20
584 Mixed Motives... 10
595 A North Country Maid. Mrs. H. Lovett Cameron... 20
599 Lancelot Ward, M.P. George Temple... 10
612 My Wife's Niece. By the author of "Dr. Edith Romney"... 20
624 Primus in Indis. M. J. Colquhoun... 10
628 Wedded Hands. Author of "My Lady's Folly"... 20
634 The Unforeseen. Alice O'Hanlon... 20
637 What's His Offence?... 20
641 The Rabbi's Spell. Stuart C. Cumberland... 10
643 The Sketch-Book of Geoffrey Crayon, Gent. Washington Irving... 20
644 A Girton Girl. Mrs. Annie Edwards... 20
652 The Lady with the Rubies. E. Marlitt... 20
654 "Us." An Old-fashioned Story. Mrs. Molesworth... 10
662 The Mystery of Allan Grale. Isabella Fyvie Mayo... 20
668 Half-Way. An Anglo-French Romance... 20
669 The Philosophy of Whist. By William Pole... 20
675 Mrs. Dymond. Miss Thackeray 20
679 Where Two Ways Meet. Sarah Doudney... 10
681 A Singer's Story. May Laffan. 10
683 The Bachelor Vicar of Newforth. Mrs. J. Harcourt-Roe. 20
684 Last Days at Apswich... 10
692 The Mikado, and Other Comic Operas. Written by W. S. Gilbert. Composed by Arthur Sullivan... 20
705 The Woman I Loved, and the Woman Who Loved Me. By Isa Blagden... 10
706 A Crimson Stain. By Annie Bradshaw... 10
708 Ormond. By Maria Edgeworth 20
709 Zenobia; or, The Fall of Palmyra. By William Ware. 1st half... 20
709 Zenobia; or, The Fall of Palmyra. By William Ware. 2d half... 20
712 For Maimie's Sake. By Grant Allen... 20
718 Unfairly Won. By Mrs. Power O'Donoghue... 20
719 Childe Harold's Pilgrimage. By Lord Byron... 10
723 Mauleverer's Millions. By T. Wemyss Reid... 20
725 My Ten Years' Imprisonment. By Silvio Pellico... 10
730 The Autobiography of Benjamin Franklin... 10
731 The Bayou Bride. By Mrs. Mary E. Bryan... 20
735 Until the Day Breaks. By Emily Spender... 20
738 In the Golden Days. By Edna Lyall... 20
748 Hurrish: A Study. By the Hon. Emily Lawless... 20
749 Lord Vanecourt's Daughter. By Mabel Collins... 20
757 Love's Martyr. By Laurence Alma Tadema... 10
759 In Shallow Waters. By Annie Armitt... 20

The foregoing works, contained in THE SEASIDE LIBRARY, Pocket Edition, are for sale by all newsdealers, or will be sent to any address, postage free, on receipt of price. *Parties ordering by mail will please order by numbers.* Address

GEORGE MUNRO,
MUNRO'S PUBLISHING HOUSE,

P. O. Box 3751.   17 to 27 Vandewater Street, N. Y.

THE SEASIDE LIBRARY.—Pocket Edition.

LATEST ISSUES:

NO.		PRICE	NO.		PRICE
669	Pole on Whist..................	20	761	Will Weatherhelm. By Wm. H. G. Kingston..............	20
737	Aunt Rachel. By David Christie Murray.....................	10	762	Impressions of Theophrastus Such. By George Eliot.......	10
738	In the Golden Days. By Edna Lyall......................	20	763	The Midshipman, Marmaduke Merry. By Wm. H. G. Kingston	20
739	The Caged Lion. By Charlotte M. Yonge.....................	20	764	The Evil Genius. By Wilkie Collins.....................	20
740	Rhona. By Mrs. Forrester....	20	765	Not Wisely, But Too Well. By Rhoda Broughton...........	20
741	The Heiress of Hilldrop; or, The Romance of a Young Girl. By Charlotte M. Braeme, author of "Dora Thorne"...	20	766	No. XIII; or, the Story of the Lost Vestal. By Emma Marshall.....................	10
742	Love and Life. By Charlotte M. Yonge.....................	20	767	Joan. By Rhoda Broughton...	20
743	Jack's Courtship. By W. Clark Russell. 1st half..........	20	768	Red as a Rose is She. By Rhoda Broughton.................	20
743	Jack's Courtship. By W. Clark Russell. 2d half...........	20	769	Cometh Up as a Flower. By Rhoda Broughton.............	20
744	Diana Carew; or, For a Woman's Sake. By Mrs. Forrester	20	770	The Castle of Otranto. By Horace Walpole.............	10
745	For Another's Sin; or, A Struggle for Love. By Charlotte M. Braeme, author of "Dora Thorne".................	20	771	A Mental Struggle. By "The Duchess".................	20
			772	Gascoyne, the Sandal-Wood Trader. By R. M. Ballantyne	20
746	Cavalry Life; or, Sketches and Stories in Barracks and Out. By J. S. Winter..............	20	773	The Mark of Cain. By Andrew Lang.....................	10
			774	The Life and Travels of Mungo Park.....................	10
747	Our Sensation Novel. Edited by Justin H. McCarthy, M.P..	10	775	The Three Clerks. By Anthony Trollope...................	20
748	Hurrish: A Study. By the Hon. Emily Lawless..........	20	776	Père Goriot. By H. De Balzac.	20
749	Lord Vanecourt's Daughter. By Mabel Collins..................	20	777	The Voyages and Travels of Sir John Maundeville, Kt........	10
750	An Old Story of My Farming Days. By Fritz Reuter. First half.......................	20	778	Society's Verdict. By the Author of "My Marriage"...........	20
			779	Doom! An Atlantic Episode. By Justin H. McCarthy, M.P.	10
750	An Old Story of My Farming Days. By Fritz Reuter. Second half.......................	20	780	Rare Pale Margaret. By author of "What's His Offence?"....	20
752	Jackanapes, and Other Stories. By Juliana Horatia Ewing..	10	781	The Secret Dispatch. By James Grant.....................	10
753	King Solomon's Mines. By H. Rider Haggard................	20	782	The Closed Door. By F. Du Boisgobey. 1st half.........	20
754	How to be Happy Though Married. By a Graduate in the University of Matrimony.....	20	782	The Closed Door. By F. Du Boisgobey. 2d half..........	20
			783	Chantry House. By Charlotte M. Yonge.................	20
755	Margery Daw. A Novel.......	20	785	The Haunted Chamber. By "The Duchess"..............	10
756	The Strange Adventures of Captain Daugerous. A Narrative in Plain English. Attempted by George Augustus Sala....	20	787	Court Royal. A Story of Cross Currents. By S. Baring-Gould	20
757	Love's Martyr. By Laurence Alma Tadema.......	10	790	The Chaplet of Pearls; or, The White and Black Ribaumont. Charlotte M. Yonge. 1st half	20
758	"Good-bye, Sweetheart!" By Rhoda Broughton............	20	790	The Chaplet of Pearls; or, The White and Black Ribaumont. Charlotte M. Yonge. 2d half	20
759	In Shallow Waters. By Annie Armitt......................	20			
760	Aurelian; or, Rome in the Third Century. By William Ware..	20			

The foregoing works, contained in THE SEASIDE LIBRARY, Pocket Edition, are for sale by all newsdealers, or will be sent to any address, postage free, on receipt of price. *Parties ordering by mail will please order by numbers.* Address

GEORGE MUNRO,
MUNRO'S PUBLISHING HOUSE,

P. O. Box 3751.   17 to 27 Vandewater Street, N. Y.

PEARS' SOAP

A SPECIALTY FOR INFANTS

The New York Fashion Bazar.

THE BEST AMERICAN HOME MAGAZINE.
Price 25 Cents per Copy. Subscription Price $3.00 per Year.

Among its regular contributors are MARY CECIL HAY, "THE DUCHESS," author of "Molly Bawn," LUCY RANDALL COMFORT, CHARLOTTE M. BRAEME, author of "Dora Thorne," MRS. ALEX. McVEIGH MILLER, MARY E. BRYAN, author of "Manch," and FLORENCE A. WARDEN, author of "The House on the Marsh."

COMMENTS OF THE PRESS:

THE NEW YORK FASHION BAZAR aims to give full information of what ladies and children should wear, and, from the space devoted to the matter, both pictorially and descriptively, we would suppose it succeeds. There is also a considerable amount of miscellaneous reading matter, especially of fiction. (Published by George Munro, New York City. $3.00 a year.)—*United Presbyterian.*

THE NEW YORK FASHION BAZAR for this month, George Munro, publisher, is on our table, and an interesting number it is to the women of the land who have their spring costumes to make up. This magazine is standard and the best authority on matters of fashion.—*Baptist Reflector.*

THE current number of THE NEW YORK FASHION BAZAR, published by George Munro, New York, is an illustrated library, as it were, of fashions in every branch of human wear. The figures, forms, and fittings are almost bewildering even to those who possess a quick eye to the subject that is so widely fascinating. The colored first page of the cover is too attractive to such people to be resisted. The Fashion Colored Supplement forms the frontispiece to the present number.—*New England Journal of Agriculture.*

WE have received the last number of THE NEW YORK FASHION BAZAR, published by George Munro, New York City, the yearly subscription of which is only $3. Each number has a large colored fashion supplement, containing New York and Paris fashions, and the book is full of illustrations of every conceivable article of ladies' attire and descriptions how to make the same, besides serial stories and sketches and much miscellaneous matter.—*Maine Farmer.*

WE have received the last number of THE NEW YORK FASHION BAZAR, and at a hasty glance we see it is an interesting magazine. Its fashions are useful to those ladies who do their own dressmaking, or even decide how they shall be made, and its stories are fascinating. What more can we say? Address George Munro, 17 Vandewater Street, N. Y.—*Worcester [Mass.] Chronicle.*

THE NEW YORK FASHION BAZAR, published by George Munro, is full of fashions and reading. It seems to be very full, and to be well adapted to the end sought. The yearly subscription is $3.00, or 25 cents a number. It is very large, containing seventy-four pages, large size.—*Wilmington Morning Star.*

THE NEW YORK FASHION BAZAR contains an attractive variety of literary entertainments, stories, poems, sketches, etc., in addition to the display of ladies' fashions which are its chief study. These are set forth with an array of pictures and descriptions which should leave nothing to doubt regarding the newest styles. The selection of embroidery patterns offers a tempting choice for artistic tastes. New York: George Munro. — *Home Journal.*

THE NEW YORK FASHION BAZAR, with supplement, is one of the most interesting and ornamental periodicals that have reached the *Herald* office. It is issued by the publisher of the *Fireside Companion* and *Seaside Library.*—*Chicago Herald.*

THE NEW YORK FASHION BAZAR, published by George Munro, for this month, is a marvel of beauty and excellence. It is full of entertaining reading, and of the newest and most fashionable patterns and designs. It must be seen to be appreciated.—*Church Press.*

THE NEW YORK FASHION BAZAR is for sale by all newsdealers, price 25 cents per copy. Subscription price $3.00 per year. Address

GEORGE MUNRO, Munro's Publishing House,

P. O. Box 3751.   17 to 27 Vandewater Street, N. Y.

THE CELEBRATED
SOHMER

GRAND, SQUARE AND UPRIGHT PIANOS.

FIRST PRIZE DIPLOMA.

Centennial Exhibition, 1876; Montreal, 1881 and 1882.

The enviable position Sohmer & Co. hold among American Piano Manufacturers is solely due to the merits of their instruments.

They are used in Conservatories, Schools and Seminaries, on account of their superior tone and unequaled durability.

The SOHMER Piano is a special favorite with the leading musicians and critics.

ARE AT PRESENT THE MOST POPULAR AND PREFERRED BY THE LEADING ARTISTS.

SOHMER & CO., Manufacturers, No. 149 to 155 E. 14th Street, N. Y.

6,000 MILES OF RAILROAD

THE BEST IN THE WORLD

IT TRAVERSES THE MOST DESIRABLE PORTIONS OF

ILLINOIS, IOWA, NEBRASKA, WISCONSIN, MINNESOTA, DAKOTA AND NORTHERN MICHIGAN.

THE POPULAR SHORT LINE

BETWEEN

| CHICAGO, | MILWAUKEE, | MADISON, | ST. PAUL, | MINNEAPOLIS, |
| OMAHA, | COUNCIL BLUFFS, | | DENVER, | SAN FRANCISCO, |

PORTLAND, OREGON,

AND ALL POINTS IN THE WEST AND NORTHWEST.

PALACE ✧ SLEEPING ✧ CARS, ✧ PALATIAL ✧ DINING ✧ CARS

AND SUPERB DAY COACHES ON THROUGH TRAINS.

Close connections in Union depots with branch and connecting lines

ALL AGENTS SELL TICKETS VIA THE NORTH-WESTERN.

New York Office, 409 Broadway. Chicago Office, 62 Clark St. Denver Office, 8 Windsor Hotel Block.
Boston Office, 5 State Street. Omaha Office, 1411 Farnam St. San Francisco Office, 2 New Montgomery St.
Minneapolis Office, 13 Nicollet House. St. Paul Office, 159 E. Third St. Milwaukee Office, 102 Wisconsin Street.

R. S. HAIR, General Passenger Agent, CHICAGO, ILL.

www.ingramcontent.com/pod-product-compliance
Lightning Source LLC
Chambersburg PA
CBHW030305170426
43202CB00009B/879